To Sam
with best wishes,

Maxine

Mindful
of
the *Miracle*

A MEMOIR

Mannie Stein

MALCOLM LESTER

National Library of Canada Cataloguing in Publication

Stein, Mannie, 1920–
    Mindful of the miracle : a memoir / Mannie Stein.

ISBN 0-9689415-2-4

1. Stein, Mannie, 1920– 2. Surgeons—South Africa—Biography.
3. Jews—Canada—Biography. I. Title.

RD27.35.S74A3 2003   617'.092   C2003-904306-1

Book Design: Jack Steiner

Printed and bound in Canada

03 04   3 2 1

*This book is dedicated
to my late wife,
Lola,
whose love,
dignity, spirit,
and smile
were my inspiration*

Acknowledgments

I must give credit to my son, Mike, whose constant nagging to write my memoirs finally wore me down. This is the result. Without his desire to have a written biography for the sake of the family, I would never have put pen to paper. Now, as I see the final result, I thank him very much and hope that it gives him as much pleasure as it does me.

Further credit must go to Mordechai and Lynn Ben Dat, whose help and guidance shaped this autobiography. I could not have done it alone. They gave of their time and knowledge unstintingly and have now become true and loving friends.

I thank Malcolm Lester for all his help and advice in bringing this book to fruition.

My thanks also go to my editor, Andrea Knight, who spent days in correcting my errors.

Last, but not least, my thanks go to Jack Steiner, the designer, who created such an appealing book.

Contents

Foreword

WHEN THE AMERICAN WRITER and philosopher, Ralph Waldo Emerson, wrote "there is properly no history, only biography," he could have been thinking of Mannie Stein. But had Emerson known Stein, he would have been doubly pleased—pleased at the acquaintanceship with so rare an individual and pleased that the truth of his aphorism could be so splendidly affirmed.

The meaning of Emerson's aphorism, of course, is that in every generation, there are certain individuals whose lives sparkle, like refracted light, through the many swirling, epochal currents of human history.

Mannie Stein is one of those individuals.

Spanning four continents and more than four score years, his life has been a veritable mirror shining back the light of countless personal achievements and the larger, stirring events of a hopeful humanity. Written humbly, perhaps even with excessive deference to modesty, Stein's autobiography tells the story of that life.

He was one of the pioneers of vascular surgery in South Africa during the turbulent middle years of the last century. One of the youngest, if not the youngest, person ever to graduate from medical school in South Africa, he helped advance the frontiers of healing. He took risks. He innovated. He brilliantly and uniquely combined the empiricism of the science he was taught with the metaphysics of the art that was in his soul. Healing was the calling to which he responded with a zealot's passion and a father's love.

But medicine and vascular surgery were merely the central pre-occupations of Stein's life; they were not nearly its totality.

Mannie Stein's life is also a fractal of physics and geometry, a miniature of the full imprint of Jewish migration, community, and peoplehood during the last century.

The story of his life begins in a dirt-road village in Lithuania. Through achievement and excellence, reward and recognition, travail and tears, it led him to Africa, to Israel, and is now winding down in Canada. Like his autobiography, Mannie Stein is understated and elegant. That I am able to say I am his friend is a generosity from on High and a blessing for which I will always be grateful.

Mordechai Ben-Dat
Editor, *The Canadian Jewish News*
Toronto, April 2003

Prologue

IT WASN'T A PARTICULARLY rowdy night. Activity on the street outside the hospital seemed no more heated than normal. It was summer and most of the people in the neighbourhood were escaping the sultry squalor of their homes by seeking the occasional cooling breezes of the sidewalks. We were on duty, as usual, in the casualty ward of Coronation Hospital, tending to the various medical emergencies that the steamy summer nights visited upon the bodies of the black men and women in this southern suburb of Johannesburg.

Coronation Hospital is a teaching hospital for black patients and all doctors affiliated with the University of Witwatersrand. At the time, it had two surgical units that alternated weekdays of intake with weekends on duty. Each unit had a chief, a registrar (resident), and a houseman (intern). There was no assistant chief in the units, which meant that the registrar had to bear more responsibility than the norm. What the chief didn't do, the registrar did.

I was the registrar on call that night.

The hospital served the surrounding black townships as well as a coloured township. Violence was rife in the area. On any weekend we would deal with forty to fifty stab wounds in the chest, as well as fractured skulls, jaws, arms, legs, and a multitude of other trauma injuries.

Some hours after my shift began, past midnight in the early morning of that hot summer night, I was summoned from the upstairs lounge by a sister whose controlled call of distress left no doubt in my mind that I was needed immediately.

When I got to the ward, I found, sitting upright in a chair, eyes wide open, hands placidly at his side, a man with the blade of a large knife lodged deeply into the middle of his skull, the broken wooden handle of the weapon protruding straight up in the air like a miniature fencepost stuck in thick mud. Incredibly, he had walked into the ward under his own strength and was fully conscious, ready to tell us what had happened. But the story of how the knife became lodged in his brain was less compelling to me than the need to immediately extract it, which would not be that simple. The knife was in the central area of the brain where a large vein ran; in effect, it was acting like a cork, stemming the flow of blood. To control the bleeding as the knife blade was extracted, it would be necessary to raise a flap of bone.

There were very few neurosurgeons in South Africa in those days; general surgeons treated all the "routine" brain trauma. Needless to say, in this case, we had to act quickly. I decided not to pull the knife out, at least not yet. It was lodged squarely on the sagittal sinus, the main vein between the two cranial hemispheres. Were I to yank the knife out without first establishing some control over that vein, the man would die within minutes, before we could open his skull. We would have to make an incision in the skull on either side of the knife blade that was large enough for us to see exactly how the blade was lodged; from there we could determine how best to remove it.

We rushed our patient to the operating theatre, anesthetized him, and proceeded to open his skull. We created a flap of skin and bone from the skull and lifted it to expose all of the knife. As we removed the knife, I put my thumb on the sagittal sinus and took some temporal side muscle to use as a plug to stop the bleeding in the spot from which the knife had been removed. I waited and waited until the bleeding stopped. Once it did, we put the flap of skin and bone back in its place in the man's skull. It was a tight fit. Eventually the skin grew back over the flap, sealing the removed portion of the skull back into its former place.

The entire procedure had taken only 45 minutes.

More than a half century later, in the study of my home in Toronto, at a remove both of great distance and time, I recall that surrealistic post-midnight moment in Johannesburg. That bizarre scene in the hospital, much like the broken-handled knife at its centre, is deeply embedded into my memory. I reach for it. Along with countless other scenes, inside and outside the hospital, they form the tale of a life lived by a surgeon.

I feel the urge now, for my sake, if not for posterity, and for all those whom I have loved and still do, to try to tell that tale. It began, as it did for most of the Jews of South Africa, in Lithuania.

"Thank you seems quite inadequate to express
my deep appreciation and gratitude to you and
that wonderful team which helped to perform
what to me and mine will always be a miracle.
For this alone, I am deeply indebted
and how much more so
by your wonderful generosity."
—REV. HUGH F. YULE, AUGUST 1962

Chapter 1

Lithuania

I WAS BORN IN BALNINKAI—Baulnik, as it was known among Jews—in Lithuania, a few days after Pesach (Passover) 1920. Like many people born in the small shtetlach of eastern Europe, I do not know the exact date of my birth. As a result, I celebrate my birthday on April 1. I have no memories of my birthplace because we left there when I was a year old to take up residence in Vilkomir (Ukmerga), a much larger city of about 10,500—a short trip by cattle-drawn cart—northeast of Kaunas (Kovno). Some 3,885 Ukmergans, or 37.5 per cent, were Jews, making the city a major Jewish community in Lithuania. During the 1920s, the 153,000 Jews of Lithuania were that country's largest national minority, comprising just over 7 per cent of the total population—a fact that so bothered some Lithuanian nationalists that, barely two decades later, they willingly, indeed unabashedly, joined forces with the Nazis.

My earliest memories are of our home in Vilkomir.

My parents, Malka and Yudel (Yehuda), and my mother's parents, Havis and Shayna Hackner, lived in a small single-storey wood-frame house with a very little front yard. Down the hill, on a narrow dirt road about twenty-five metres from our house, was the mikveh that my father, and I presume my mother in her turn as well, used regularly. Further down the hill was a little stream along whose rock-strewn edges my brother, my friends, and I used to play.

When I visited Vilkomir in 1996 with two of my children and some friends, I was able to find my way back to that stream and even to the mikveh, which is still standing, though dilapidated and ramshackle, and, of course, no longer in use.

The images and colours of home that so impressed the psyche of a young five- or six-year-old seem rather dark and dull to me today. There is a picture in my mind: the front door is open and an old man with a long grey beard is sitting far back in the small entrance hall, off to one side. That man was my maternal grandfather. All I remember of him is that he was always praying, studying, and reading from the holy texts, and that he suffered from high blood pressure and related heart problems—he kept a container of *pyofkes* (leeches) on a bench next to him. As was an accepted treatment then, the leeches were used to suck out small amounts of blood that would thereby help to reduce his blood pressure. I remember those leeches vividly owing to a prank I once played on my grandfather. I thought it would amuse him—to a five-year-old, it seemed very funny to let the leeches out of their container. My grandfather, however, was not amused. I do not recall if my grandmother was as upset with me as my grandfather was, but I do remember that my brother Morris, two years older than me, agreed that my prank was pretty funny.

Looking back on my encounter with my grandfather's leeches, it's probably true to say that it was my introduction to medicine, which became my life's calling.

I have no recollection whatsoever of my father's parents.

My parents, Malka and Yudel, had a wholesale soft goods, or textiles, business that I think my mother mostly ran. My father was more a scholar than a businessman. He mastered many languages: Yiddish, the language we spoke at home, Hebrew, Lithuanian, Russian, Polish, German, and later in South Africa, English and Zulu.

Our home was modest, but, as was typical of shtetl life, it was also warm and sustaining. My mother was a very good cook whose skills were put to delightful, sumptuous use on Shabbat and holidays, the centrepieces of our family occasions. Festive meals were feasts—soup, borscht, *gehackteh lebber* (chopped liver), *lokshen* and potato puddings, chicken, and, always served last, *gribones* (fried chicken fat). It was indeed a culinary delight, in no small part, probably, because it was also a cholesterol nightmare.

In the summer my mother would take Morris and me into the nearby forest to pick berries. The forest was vast and magical. Those summertime forays stay with me as the highlight of my few youthful years in Vilkomir.

Of course, we went to cheder in Vilkomir, but I do not recall too much from those days.

Pogroms against Jews had abated by the 1920s, but anti-Semitism had not. Jews were always looking for an opportunity to emigrate to the West. However, it was very difficult to get immigration papers. Fortunately for us, some of my mother's brothers had emigrated to South Africa a few years earlier and one of them, Sam, was able to sponsor us.

My mother had seven brothers, Moshe, Micha, Kay, Abraham, Leizer, Sam, and Oscar, and one sister, Rivka. Except for Moshe and Abraham, all of my uncles had emigrated to South Africa and had settled in Durban. Moshe's children subsequently emigrated to South Africa as well. Abraham, who was a bachelor, remained behind.

Although I was too young to have understood the true dimension of the conditions under which we lived in Lithuania, it is evident, looking back, that hardship was a constant companion. Everyone had to deal with myriad moments of adversity each day. And yet, no one was immobilized by it; no one dwelt on it. One did what was necessary to raise one's children, to support one's family. I imagine that my parents, like so many of their friends and family, made the decision to leave when economic conditions became unbearable, when social conditions became too insecure, when providing for the next day became simply too uncertain.

My uncle Leizer and his wife, Mirel, in some respects, typified the resolve and the inner strength of Lithuanian Jews. Leizer became engaged to Mirel, who was from Vilna while he was still in Vilkomir. Before they were due to marry, however, Mirel went blind. Nevertheless, they still married and eventually moved to South Africa. In South Africa, they ran a corner store and lived in the back. Despite her disability, Mirel did all the housework, which meant cooking on a coal stove. Though she burned herself many times on that stove, she carried on with her life in all aspects, an affirmation of human dignity and determination. She even bore and raised two sons. I remember going often to Uncle Leizer's store, where I would get a good meal and always be greeted by Uncle Leizer and Aunt Mirel's cheerful faces.

I do not recall the atmosphere in our home leading up to our emigration. Undoubtedly it was one of apprehension and anticipation as my parents were planning our future in a faraway place. Before our immigration papers arrived, my brother Haim was born, in December 1925. Now we were three brothers. Soon after his birth, with the sense of celebration still clinging to the walls in our home, my father left for South Africa.

What an anxious time that must have been for my mother. It is unimaginable to me today. What if something happened to my father? What if he never sent for her? What if she never heard from him again? I always felt much closer to my mother than to my father. Is it any wonder? How much of my subsequent relationship with him was influenced by the inexplicability to a five-year-old of his father's sudden departure from his wife and children?

In Durban, my father opened an eatery where blacks could get both hot and cold food and buy food supplies. That he was able to start up the business by himself, even though he did not speak any language with which he could make himself understood, was simply remarkable. After working for close to a year, sleeping on the long metal tables in his eatery, he managed to save enough money to send for his family.

After the death of her husband, my maternal grandmother also moved to South Africa for a time. My uncle Sam paid for her passage and she stayed with us. But she didn't like the new country. She couldn't or wouldn't adjust to a new way of life, new environment, new climate, new customs, new languages. So she returned to Lithuania where she died before World War II.

Our family's emigration to South Africa in 1926 followed a pattern that was common to Lithuanian Jews in the 1920s. They were driven by three factors: the economic hardships and difficulty in providing for their families, the constant physical threats to their security, and the official policy of trying to "de-Judaize" young Jewish boys by drafting them into the army for lengthy periods of service, often as long as twelve years.

❖ ❖ ❖

Some seventy years later, I returned to Lithuania.

I knew that my friend Jonathan Beare had travelled there from time to time and was involved in the religious and cultural revival of the Lithuanian Jewish community, so I approached him for information about a journey to Lithuania. My son, Mike, had discussed the possibility of our taking a trip there and I was interested in knowing more of the details. No sooner had I broached the subject with Jonathan than he was already including us in his next trip, which was imminent. He was and is that type of a person. Generosity is second nature to him. Many individuals have been the beneficiaries of his kindness, most of them never even knowing how or why, or who their benefactor was. His reputation in our community and in communities around the world as a philanthropist of countless causes, large and small, is without parallel.

Jonathan was planning a trip to Lithuania on which he was taking a rabbi from Johannesburg and the rabbi's brother from London along with him. In an instant, it was decided that Mike, his wife, Pam, and I would join them on their eight-day trip. The prospect excited me. I was deeply curious about the place that had been my first home and that had spawned the way of life that my parents had transplanted for themselves and for us in South Africa.

Jonathan described that way of life in a statement checkered with the colourful Yiddish terminology that more truly reflects the flavour of his subject. Although somewhat idealized—perhaps even sanitized—in terms of the dynamics that naturally result among individuals who are forced to live in cramped, confined, and close quarters, the underlying framework of values by which the communities lived and were governed rings true even in our own modern era.

"If there was a single thread which characterized every shtetl in Lithuania, it was the fact that the Jews lived in poverty. Simple people, who didn't have two rubles to rub together, lived beautiful family lives where the meat on the table and the fancy clothes were replaced with great *yiras Shamayim* (fear of God) and *ahavas Yisroel* (love for their fellow Jews). The smallest shtetl, while lacking in all materiality, was sure to have a *gemillus chessed* (a philanthropic society), a *chevras bikkur cholim* (an association to visit the sick), a *chevras hachnosses kallah* (an association to assist young women to marry), a *chevrah kadisha* (a burial society) and many other institutions. *Shtetl mentschen* (people), whether they were *baal melochehs* (artisans such as carpenters and shoemakers) or whether they were *soichers* (merchants) dealing in wood, flour, or flax, or whether they were shopkeepers, were more often than not steeped in learning. A Jew may have been lacking in *parnosseh* (income), but in learning, very few of these humble people lacked the knowledge of Torah and Talmud. The value system by which they conducted their lives was based on traditional Jewish values as practised by observant Jews throughout history."

I am generally not an emotional individual, nor do I tend to wax sentimental in front of others. For most of my life, dispassion has been my reigning emotion. And although dispassion in high-pressure surgical situations or other taut medical crises is always helpful, I cannot attribute that trait to my training as a surgeon. It is simply my nature to be more private and more controlled in my emotions. But the trip to Lithuania surprised me. I did not expect to react the way that I did. There were some moments of great emotion that would have been foolish and vain to try to hide.

Wherever we travelled, I visualized my parents walking on the landscape. As soon as we arrived at my childhood home in Vilkomir, the image of my grandfather filled my mind's eye. I could see him again, with his long, grey beard, in the narrow corridor of our home, sitting, slightly hunched over, typically with a book in his hand, reading, learning, or praying.

We went to Vilna and Kovno. In every community we visited, hospitality was effusive, due entirely to Jonathan's presence on our tour. He was quite renowned in Lithuania because of his long-standing involvement with the various communities there. We were invited out for dinner every night. And the menu was a delight to my palate. It stirred my taste buds as well as my memory. It was the food of my youth, the food of my mother's kitchen: *gribones, gehackteh lebber,* and *taigelach* (honey-dipped pastries). We drove from one end of the country to the other. We made a point of visiting Zagor, my father-in-law's home town, and Memel, where Pam's grandmother came from.

Despite the passage of time, the material and scientific progress, and the advancements in Western technology, much of what we saw in Lithuania seemed stuck in the past. It was easy to see myself as a youngster running on the unpaved street in front of our house, getting into some sort of mischief. The manner of life of my family and other Jewish families a hundred years ago came alive in my mind. The tombstones in the cemeteries were especially fascinating for me. As I read the names I better understood the interconnectedness of Jewish life and Jewish history. Virtually all of the names I read on the cold stone markers were recognizable in South Africa, indeed anywhere in the world where Ashkenazi Jews have lived. I could also imagine more clearly—and thus fathom perhaps for truly the first time—the sheer courage and profound will of our forebears who travelled vast distances under conditions of severe hardship to build better lives for their families.

At the end of each day, the six of us would set aside a few moments to reflect on the day's experiences and sights. We had a great many philosophical discussions during the trip, lasting long into the night, on subjects that ranged from current and past politics, Jewish and general history, Israel, the Diaspora, Jewish peoplehood to religion, and Jewish observance. We had become a tight and close-knit group, each caring for the other. It was interesting to observe the social transformation of the two brothers. At the outset, the men, both of whom were observant, tended to keep their distance from Pam. Due to religious strictures, they were reluctant to sit near her or engage her too pointedly in our regular debates or join in the singing—that we often did around the various tables to which we were invited each night—when her voice could be heard in the group as well. But by trip's end, the physical closeness of the group had fostered an emotional and intellectual closeness as well. The two men had fully adjusted to Pam's proximity and actively invited her full and equal participation in the trip's many social and other delights. Their inhibitions softened to the point where they would ask Pam to add a harmony or strengthen the melodies of the Yiddish *nigunim* (tunes) that poured out of their souls each night.

"When a brilliant surgeon, such as yourself, has saved the life of someone very precious and dear, it is very hard to put into words the gratitude one feels. We are fully aware of the fact that but for your prompt action and wonderful surgery, Father would not have come back to us last Thursday. We are so deeply grateful for all you have done and for your wonderful aftercare and your unfailing patience. Your quiet confidence and your reassurance to my mother on the night of the operation was greatly appreciated... God bless you in your work and we do thank God for brilliant surgeons like you."

—JOSÉ MUNRO, MAY 1962

CHAPTER 2

Journey to South Africa

I WAS SIX WHEN MY MOTHER GATHERED up her children and took us from Lithuania to South Africa. Morris was eight; Hymie (Haim) was not even a year old. I remember the departure from Vilkomir's train station. My memories are only of my mother, of her crying, of her repeatedly kissing my grandmother, my grandfather, and my aunt. Although I was distressed at seeing my mother so sad, so tearful, I was far too young to be aware of how emotional that moment must have been for her. She would never see her father or her sister again.

But there was precious little opportunity for her to dwell on her emotions. She had to tend to her three young children. She managed to organize everything for our comfort during that trip. We were all in one compartment:—my mother, my two brothers, and I—and all our *pecklech* (packages), the eiderdown comforters, the clothing, the kosher food, of which there were numerous tins and jars, as well as the kosher dishes.

That train took us and our *pecklech* to Hamburg where we boarded what seemed to me an enormous ship.

I liked being on the ship. Though I spoke only Yiddish and Lithuanian, I do not recall language posing a problem. Morris and I hung around together. It was a playful adventure for a six-year-old. The purser took a liking to me and brought me chocolate puddings, which I remember enjoying a great deal, although I never told my mother about his generosity. It was my first taste of non-kosher food. Otherwise, all our food came from the stores my mother had brought on board, along with the crockery in which to heat it, the plates on which to put it, and the cutlery with which to eat it. When we entered the dining room, we brought our own kitchen with us.

When I think back on that trip, I am amazed at what an onerous undertaking it must have been for my mother travelling alone with three such young children—two young boys, who, though somewhat bashful, were still full of discovery and youthful mischief, keen on having the run of the ship, and the third an infant under one year of age. I have no unpleasant recollections of that voyage, which is a tribute both to how the passage of time can smooth the jagged edges of memory and to my mother's remarkable endurance and affection.

After a long journey at sea, we landed in Cape Town where we were met by representatives of the Jewish community. The ship then continued on to Durban, docking at the Point, as the harbour was called. My father and other members of the family met us there. I was a shy little boy and undoubtedly met the greeting party clinging to my brother's hand or my mother's skirt. My response to seeing my father again must have disappointed him as being excessively reserved. But what was I to do? It had been a year since I had seen him. And everything, including him, seemed so strange.

We were now in a new world.

Durban is on the Indian Ocean and is the largest port in South Africa, with a big beautiful bay and a large island in the middle called Salisbury Island. One could almost walk across the bay to the island at low tide, as we frequently did when we were young. It was a brightly lit, colourful setting—a far cry from the dull, darker, dour place we had just left in Lithuania.

My father rented our first home on Gale Street. It had not taken him very long to add mastery of Zulu to that of Yiddish, Hebrew, Lithuanian, Russian, and English. He chose Gale Street because it was halfway between the family business—an eatery for black workers—and the synagogue, about two kilometres away, that we attended with our father on Friday night, Shabbat, and holidays. During the week, my father would generally *daven* at home before he went off to work.

But the cost of the home was also a factor in my father's choice of location. The neighbourhood was a poorer one; the homes were less expensive. Our house was a single-storey, brick bungalow with a corrugated iron roof and plenty of land around it. It had running water, but the taps of the sink provided only cold water. We boiled the water in pots on the coal stove in the kitchen to get hot water. There was no indoor toilet. Although we had electricity, we often had to rely on candles and paraffin lamps. Not only did the electricity frequently fail, but we had to conserve its use because of cost. The light we did have in the house came from a single bulb dangling on a cord from the ceiling.

The toilet was in the far corner of the backyard. A sewage truck came periodically to the house at night to collect the waste from the toilet and replace the pails. There was no water-borne sewage then, or septic tanks. Fortunately Durban has a very mild winter in which temperatures rarely drop below 15° Celsius. Thus an early morning or late-night trip to the toilet was not a terrible inconvenience. In any event, we always had a chamber pot under the bed. When it rained—and it rained a great deal in Durban, especially in the summer—the backyard became very muddy. The trip to the toilet was often messy. In addition, the roof of the toilet leaked. But, as we were children and had never known anything different, we did not think it a hardship.

Durban has a wonderful tropical climate. It is very hot and very humid in summer. As I have said, there is no season that Canadians would recognize as winter. I never owned, let alone wore, a coat. It was green all the time in Durban. There were myriad colourful flowers and a great variety of abundant, deeply verdant forms of other vegetation.

Of course, there was no air conditioning. We tried to make do by having the doors and windows open as much as possible. We even kept the windows open at night. But the mosquitoes and flies were a problem, so we used metal mesh to cover any food that was exposed to the air.

Ensuring that various foodstuffs and milk products did not spoil was a major concern because we had no refrigerator. To prevent spoilage we acquired an icebox and cooled the food with blocks of ice that we transported to our home on rickshaws. The blocks of the ice would then be chipped into sizes that fit into the icebox chest.

The rickshaw was a means of transportation for people as well as for blocks of ice. In Durban in the late 1920s, it was a common form of carriage and remained so for many years. The haulers of rickshaws were mainly Zulus who dressed up with headdresses and ankle ornaments that made a jingling noise when they moved. These men had tremendous stamina and could pull the rickshaws for miles without stopping. When they worked on the beachfront, they decorated the headdresses with multicoloured plumage and large horns. This was done to attract tourists. As the years went by, the transport rickshaws gradually disappeared until only a few remained for the occasional beachfront visitor.

The Indian market was already an institution in Durban. I vividly remember going there as a youngster with my mother every Friday morning to buy fresh fruit, vegetables, and the odd live chicken. We looked upon a trip to the Indian market as a great treat. The chaos, the noise, the aromas were all very striking, a veritable carnival of sound, colour, and smell and a delightful adventure for newly arrived immigrants from the more austere markets of Vilkomir, Lithuania. All the provisions we bought were piled into a rickshaw and hauled to our home.

Durban, then as now, was a community of three main groups: white, black, and Indian. The whites were mainly of English extraction and in the 1930s comprised about 250,000 people. The blacks came mainly from Zulu lands abutting Durban and comprised about 300,000 people. The Indians were a majority of approximately 450,000. For the most part, they were the sons and daughters of indentured workers who had come from India years before to work in the sugar fields and stayed on. The Indians developed their own community with their own schools, institutions, and organizations and many of them achieved great success in business. Mahatma Gandhi lived and worked in Durban as a young lawyer for a number of years before returning to India where he would eventually lead his countrymen to independence from the United Kingdom. Regrettably, I never met him.

The blacks were prevented from achieving the same measure of success as the Indians by the obstacles the government placed in their path. At the time, the government in Pretoria was led by the United Party, mostly English-speaking as opposed to Afrikaans-speaking, comprised of members of both British descent and Afrikaner descent. It ordained that black children would be taught in a separate education system with a different curriculum from that of the whites and Indians. Their totally inferior education system even fell under a different department, the Department of Bantu Education. The majority of blacks at that time received no education at all. This only began to change in the mid-1940s.

I had never seen a black person in Lithuania. But from the very outset of our arrival in Durban, we employed a young black—called a "pickaninny," meaning young boy—to do odd jobs around the house. All whites, regardless of their income, employed blacks, or in more accurate parlance, had black servants.

These servants lived in shacks at the back of the houses and were given food supplies, the principal staple being a finely ground oatmeal-like corn or maize called "mealie meal," from which they made their own meals, especially the main dish called *putu*. In those early years, I do not recall servants receiving a wider variety of foodstuffs such as meat, fish, eggs, butter, margarine, tea, or coffee. That changed, of course, as the years went by. Meat, fish, and other foods were added, but the mealie meal, grains, corn, and beans were still included.

Even though I was just a lad when I arrived, more than the climate was a shock to my system. The relations between blacks and whites was something completely new to me. It is an understatement, but certainly no less true to say that blacks were very deferential to whites. We were called "boss." Age did not matter. Even if he was twenty years older than I, a black man would still call me boss. He would automatically step off the pavement when he saw a white man walking toward him, without any instruction from the white man or even a desire on the part of the white man that the black man do so. Such was their conditioning at the time.

After we were well settled in Durban, my mother employed two servants.

"I realize that in your capacity as a surgeon, you have to keep
yourself immune to the personal troubles of others,
but at a time when [my husband] admitted to you that we
could not meet further obligations with regards to a fee for
another operation, you were humane to see it through without
remuneration.
"In a world that is fast becoming blasé we always strived
to keep our sincerity and we were always grateful
for your understanding."
—RENEE ASCAM, APRIL 1966

CHAPTER 3

Early days in Durban

LIKE ALL NEW IMMIGRANTS, our family struggled to make a living. We didn't have a car at that time, nor even a bicycle. My brother Morris and I were both put into Class 1 at McDonald Road Primary School. I was six years old and he was eight, but no one had prepared us for the experience. The teacher taught in English and we didn't understand a word. Yiddish was our home language. We stood out like sore thumbs. We not only sounded different, with heavily accented foreign-sounding voices, but we also looked different because we were still wearing the funny-looking, eastern-European-style school pants that reached just below the knee.

After not too much time, though, we caught on to the language and the way to dress and to our life in sunny, green, full-of-light Durban. At the end of six months, we spoke fluent English and we completed two grades in one year.

The following year we changed schools. We went to Gale Street School for Standard 1 (Grade 3). Most of our classmates there still considered us foreigners, so they discriminated against us and took out their schoolyard cruelties on us.

I was small for my age and a year younger than most of the children in my class, whereas Morris was a year older than most of the class. He was very strong for his age and a bit of a "toughie." He was always my guardian—my bodyguard, as it were—ready and able to defend me whenever needed. Unfortunately, at the beginning at least, the need arose frequently. One day, the whole schoolyard of boys, or so it seemed, piled into Morris and me, the two new kids with the strange and irritating accents. But Morris's size and strength stood him in good stead. He gave back more than he got. Thankfully, though, despite his strength and courage, a teacher came to our rescue. From then on, the taunters and teasers and other childhood menaces who lurked around building corners in the protection of their gangs left us alone.

Over the years, that incident has remained with me not only as a testament of my older brother's reliability and bravery, but also as an insight of sorts into the vulnerability of the stranger. The schoolyard and neighbourhood playgrounds can be harsh, painful proving grounds.

Morris and I remained at that school through the end of Standard 2 (Grade 4 in Canada). I finished with 97 per cent; my brother Morris with 93 per cent. Our grades were much higher than the rest of the class; we had done quite well for new kids. Then we moved to Mansfield Road School, an academically more challenging school, skipping Standard 3 (Grade 5) and going directly into Standard 4 (Grade 6). (Standard 10 is the year of matriculation, the equivalent of Grade 12 in Canada today.)

About this time we moved into a new, larger, more comfortable home on Davenport Road. My mother's younger brother, Oscar Hackner, helped us with the down payment. I still remember the cost of the house: £1,500.

This house was also a single-storey dwelling, but it had an attic room with glass windows all around that we rented out for long periods to help pay the mortgage. The house had a large kitchen with a coal stove, three bedrooms, a living room, and dining room. Its key feature for me was the indoor toilet. What luxury! Apparently, the house had been built by a very wealthy man. We had a small front garden and a large back garden, perhaps 400 square metres in size, where grapes grew across a large trellis. The servants' quarters were tucked away in a corner at the back. By this time we employed two servants, our pickaninny and one other.

When we acquired the new house, we also acquired a cow. That meant, of course, that we always had fresh milk. We also had a chicken coop in which we kept approximately a dozen birds at all times. From time to time, we even had a turkey. On Friday mornings the *shoichet* came to the house to perform his ritual duties, so that we always had fresh chicken for the Friday night Shabbat dinner. By 1932, however, my family had decided to give up the cow, the chickens, and the grapes to gain more space in the yard. This finally left me and my brothers room to play cricket and kick a ball around, which resulted in the occasional broken window.

For some reason that is unclear to me even today, I had all my teeth pulled when we moved into our own home. The extractions were performed in the house. I lay on my mother's bed while the doctor administered the general anesthetic which, at that time, consisted of a cloth placed over my face and chloroform being poured over it. The dentist then extracted my teeth.

My brother Havis was born in 1930 on the very bed that had been the operating theatre for my dental surgery. I stood on a chair to see through the fanlight above the door and watched him emerge into our world.

By the early 1930s, our financial situation had improved considerably. My father acquired a second business to go along with the eatery—a nearby corner store that was essentially run by my mother. Each of the stores was approximately 1.5 kilometres from our house and my parents walked to work.

As a result of the improvement in the family's finances, my parents sent Morris and me to Durban Boys' High School for Standard 7 (Grade 9). Even though it was a public school, a small fee was required. This was the most prestigious school in Durban and remains so to this day. Discipline was strict and included a dress code of slacks, blazer, tie, and straw basher—or boater—hat. Athletics and sports—cricket in the summer and rugby in the winter—were compulsory. Other sports such as tennis, swimming, and boxing were also available. We were put into teams and played both interschool and interprovincial matches. Unfortunately, our sporting activities were severely restricted because my father insisted we go to Hebrew classes at the synagogue every day after school.

Most of the students at Durban Boys' High School came from the Durban Preparatory High School. Morris and I came from Mansfield. As a result we were put into the lowest class—E level—of our grade. The following year, however, in Standard 8 (Grade 10), we were place in the B-level class. In Standard 9, I was placed into the A-level class. When it came time to write our matriculation exams in the last year of high school, I finished with a first-class mark with honours distinctions in mathematics and science. I was always excited by mathematics and, oddly enough, by Latin, in which I excelled as well.

A minimum of six subjects were compulsory including English and Afrikaans. I never really had problems at school. I could do my homework quickly and remembered things well, having been blessed with an almost photographic memory.

I had long ago stopped thinking of myself as an immigrant. At our very young ages, it was so easy for me and my brothers to acclimatize to our new society. Nonetheless there were always reminders that set us apart from the majority. For example, the Jews in our high school always stood in a line outside the classroom in the morning waiting for the Lord's Prayer to end before we entered class. The school was opposed to this procedure; it wanted us to join all the other white—that is, Christian—

students at first sound of the bell. But the rabbis convinced the authorities that it was inappropriate for us to do so. We weren't always comfortable with the differential treatment, but it was important to our parents, who were observant of religious custom and code in the way they had been in Lithuania.

I enjoyed high school. Most of my memories from that period and place have now been burnished into fond ones. Many years later, when my brother Hymie's classmate and family friend, Aaron Klug, was being honoured at the Durban Jewish Club for having won the prestigious Nobel Prize for chemistry, my old Latin teacher, Bill Bowdon, who had also been Klug's former teacher, told me that Klug and I were the only students he recalled from our academic year.

Klug's future could have been predicted. He was so very talented. He is now Lord Aaron and lives in Cambridge. In Latin class, he could write out a translation even while the teacher was reciting the original English prose. He was like that in every subject, receiving six distinctions in his matriculation year. He completed his BA at the age of eighteen and his honours degree at nineteen. He then achieved a master's degree and was offered a scholarship at Oxford. While he was studying at Oxford, his father would visit our house and with head in hands cry, "I still have to support my son; what will he ever do with science?"

From Oxford, Aaron was invited to attend Cambridge where he did his ground-breaking scientific work on genetic engineering, taking a nucleus from one cell and putting it into another. Some years later, one of the leading American universities attempted to recruit him to its faculty with extremely generous offers of salary and staffing for his research. But he turned down the offer and has stayed on at Cambridge University.

My companions from high school became life-long friends. My cousins Stanley and Gerald Hackner, and friends Mickey and Jackie Schaffer, and I used to watch cricket matches together. Mickey and Jackie's youngest brother, Morris, would run after us and we were reluctant to allow him to join us. But his mother would forbid us from going altogether unless we also brought Morris along. To this day, Morris Schaffer is one of my very closest friends.

At first, there was only one shul in Durban, on St. Andrews Street. It soon became apparent, however, that its members, Jews of longer standing in Durban, were not comfortable with Jews who appeared too Jewish. Nor did they like Jews to sound too foreign. It was inevitable, therefore, that some of the newcomers, including my father, Orthodox in his observance and sounding very Jewish with his heavy eastern-European accent, broke away and built their own shul on Park Street. Thus, in those early days there were two shuls in Durban: the "greener" shul on Park Street for the recently arrived immigrants and the "geller" shul on St. Andrews Street for the anglicized Durbanite Jews.

At the Park Street shul, congregants had their names on their seats. If you paid a little more you could name a seat nearer to the *Aron Kodesh* (Holy Ark). My father's seat was fairly close to the front. Upstairs was our cheder, where, each afternoon for a couple of hours after school, my brothers and I attended classes. Truth be told, we did so reluctantly because cheder took away from our sports. Nevertheless, despite our lack of enthusiasm, we dutifully went until our matriculation. My father paid a *melamed* (teacher)—Reverend Rubin, the *baal tfilah* (service reader or sexton) of the shul—to teach us our lessons. My bar mitzvah Torah portion and Haftarah (portion from the prophets) were very long. We celebrated the occasion in the usual way, with a *kiddush* (small party) in the shul and then a party at home for my friends.

Reverend Rubin was a good teacher and we were good students. I knew my *trop* (musical notes). Even as a university student, my father insisted that I read the *maftir* (Bible portion) when I returned home for holidays, and I was able to do so without any problem.

The son of our *melamed,* Mr. Rubin, incidentally, would one day became a senator and would eventually be forced to leave the country because he was an outspoken anti-apartheid proponent and too left wing for the Nationalist Party.

In 1935, I and seven others started the Habonim Youth Group in Durban. We discussed events in Palestine, studied modern Zionist history, and read Hebrew texts. We started our meetings at the Durban Jewish Club, which was run then by the geller shul. But they soon expelled us, perhaps because we were the children of members of the greener shul, or perhaps because they found our activities too Jewish. Whatever their reasons, they did not want to be associated with us. We found alternate accommodations in a little room that we let on West Street.

Then World War II broke out and everything changed.

The Jewish Club asked us to return to their premises. They wanted us back. Overnight, they had become Zionists. The club was thereafter an inviting, strongly identifying place for the Jews of the community who, in their own ways, would try to respond to the crises unfolding in Europe and Palestine. It also became a way station of hospitality for Jewish and non-Jewish soldiers and sailors who came through Durban.

My friends from Habonim were also my camping buddies: Eric and Leslie Shandel, Neville Silbert—who now lives on a *moshav* (co-operative) in Israel—and my brother Morris. On occasion we would go camping in the south, travelling by train down the coast and walking from the station to our campsite near a river bed. Of course, we did not have a tent, nor did we have any sleeping bags. We would simply put a piece of canvas over the branch of a tree and peg it into the ground to provide cover for ourselves. The "tent" was open at either end and, as long as it did not rain, we were fine. Those outings were special starlit moments. We were young and headstrong and ready to face the future.

"When we talked yesterday, I meant to tell you that,
in my opinion, I owe my life to three people—
my wife for insisting that I have a physical checkup
before leaving for Europe, Dr. Rossiter for discovering
the trouble and for sending me promptly to Mr. Stein,
and to you, Mr. Stein, for having the knowledge, skill,
and dedication to do the necessary. And, of course,
the Man Upstairs, whom you mentioned always
has a most decisive part."
—CHARLES T. CARROLL, JULY 1966

Chapter 4

Medical school

I WAS SIXTEEN YEARS OLD when I went away to medical school at the University of Witwatersrand in Johannesburg, having received a scholarship for the first year. My mother took me there. I stayed with distant relatives in Johannesburg who kept a kosher home, but they lived so far away from the school that it was problematic getting back and forth to class each day. After a couple of months, a friend in my class, Jerry Jammy, and I found accommodation much closer to the campus.

Little did I know how my life would intertwine with Jerry's again many years later. After medical school, Jerry married Bobby Nathan, whose much older brother, Boetie, had a daughter named Colleen. In 1968, Colleen married Tony Berman. Eleven years later, in 1977, Colleen developed a cancer of the stomach, which I removed for her. Unfortunately she only lived another three years and died in her early thirties. In the meantime, in 1970, my daughter, Linda, had married Anthony Schewitz. Anthony developed a lymphoma and died in 1979 at the age of forty. In 1981, Linda and Tony met and married. At the time, Tony had two small children and Linda had three. Between them they have brought up the five children. To add to the coincidence in this story, the Berman family had lived three houses away from my family in Davenport Road in Durban, yet Linda and Tony only met in 1981.

Jerry and I roomed together for the entire six years of medical school, moving over the years from place to place. Our rent was £6 s10 a month. I was getting £7 s10 a month from my parents to live on, so money was tight. My parents also arranged for us to have kosher meals.

In 1936, when I first started my training, there was no school of medicine in Durban. So, I applied to the University of the Witwatersrand because it was nearer to Durban than Cape Town. A medical school was established in Durban much later, but only for non-whites. I applied for and received a scholarship for studies in medicine based on my matric results.

I really don't know what made me go into medicine. My teachers had wanted me to pursue mathematics. But I have not a single regret over my choice. I must have been influenced by the environment created by my parents in our home, but I have no recollection of a specific event or conversation or incident that inspired me to become a doctor. I do think, however, that sixteen was too young to be starting medical school. I was somewhat immature and shy socially and small physically compared to my classmates who were all seventeen and eighteen years old. I was fortunate that the career I had chosen even at so young an age turned out to be the correct one. But most sixteen-year-olds do not have the range of experience to cope with the pressure of having to make career-path choices. Doors should never close to anyone so early in life.

Like most first-year students at university, I was surprised, if not shocked, at the teaching methods that were vastly different from what I had been accustomed to in high school. The classes were very large, the lectures very formal and dry, and the lecturers quite indifferent to us. But, also like most first-year university students, I soon adjusted and actually learned to appreciate the curriculum, if not the lectures and lecturers.

In our first year of the six-year program we studied physics, chemistry, botany, and zoology. I did very well in physics and chemistry because we had studied those subjects in high school. But I was new to botany and zoology. I wasn't much interested in botany, though I quite liked zoology since we did our own dissections. I had no difficulty passing exams because my photographic memory served me well. By 9:00 p.m. on most nights, I was able to put the books down.

Second year was the most demanding of the six years due to the volume of facts we had to learn both in anatomy and in physiology. Our professor of anatomy was Raymond Dart, a well-known anthropologist who made several discoveries regarding prehistoric man. He enjoyed toying with our minds in various ways—even suggesting that the human need for sleep was overrated. Little did we know that in subsequent years, our schedules would prove him right.

The anatomy course centred around the dissection of a cadaver. Most of the cadavers in medical school were those of black individuals; the one assigned to us was no different. There were six students per cadaver, and our lab work was often a session of sordid jokes. I did not know it then, of course, but I would soon learn that the feel of cutting into a cadaver was very different from cutting into a live patient. Over the year, I learned my anatomy well, easily adapting to the self-discipline and attention to detail that mastery of the myriad minutiae demanded.

From second year onward, classes and practicals were at the teaching hospitals that adjoined the medical school and were much closer to where I lived. There were two teaching hospitals—one for white patients and one for black patients. Segregation was the rule long before apartheid was officially legislated.

The third year of study was anchored by pathology and biochemistry. However, my academic year was disrupted by the outbreak of World War II. I will always remember where I was when we heard the news. We were sitting in the students' lounge when the voice of British Prime Minister Neville

Chamberlain came over the radio declaring war against Germany. That was September 3, 1939. Following the British declaration, our prime minister, General Jan Smuts, officially took us into the war on the side of the Allies.

Because we were already in our third year of medical studies, we were exempted from conscription. Apparently, the government determined that it was more important for the war effort that we complete our studies. I felt somewhat ambivalent about this, given what the Nazis were doing to Jews in Europe and the inherent morality of going to war to defeat the Nazis. But I stayed in school and looked for other ways to help the war effort. Many young Jews, however, did volunteer for armed service. Many, alas, did not come home. Two of my friends from Durban were among those killed in the war: Willy Hershovitz and Philly Freedman.

We had a great deal of respect for General Smuts, who at that time, was already an older man. He was prime minister when my family arrived in Durban. Smuts was highly regarded around the world. He had served in the war cabinet of Great Britain during World War I and would do so again in World War II. An intellectual, well-read person, Smuts was one of the world leaders instrumental in starting the League of Nations. In later years, when we lived in Pretoria, I would make house calls at his home in Irene, a short distance away.

General Smuts' decision to join the war on the side of Great Britain was a momentous one in South Africa and not without its complications. The Afrikaner and British South Africans were deeply divided over the war. The Afrikaners, on the whole, were opposed. Their sympathies, if not loyalties, were with the German cause. They felt great antipathy towards the British homeland. The Nationalist Party gave voice to this opposition. General Smuts, leader of the United Party, and himself an

Afrikaner, ignored the Nationalist Afrikaner call for neutrality, although not before he had agreed to certain compromises. All soldiers would be conscripted, but not all conscripts would have to fight against the Axis armies. Some Afrikaners in the army elected to serve as a militia home guard while other South Africans fought alongside the Allies in North Africa. To distinguish the two forces, the soldiers who actually fought up north wore a special orange flash shoulder stripe on their shirts.

During the war, an underground movement of pro-Nazis sympathizers and thugs tried to disrupt the country's war effort. Groups like the Greyshirts, based in Pietermaritzburg, were very active. Led by Robey Leibrandt, a former light heavyweight boxer, the Greyshirts were outspokenly anti-Semitic. It would subsequently come to light that Leibrandt had been trained in subversion and sabotage in Germany and then dropped off the coast of Southwest Africa. His bullies and hoodlums were known to deface Jewish cemeteries and synagogues. The police, who were mainly Afrikaners, were generally ineffective in bringing Leibrandt's crude hooligans to a halt because they tended to support Leibrandt's views. As a result, out of sheer necessity, a group of young Jewish men banded together in Durban to protect Jewish property and holy sites and to oppose the Greyshirts. This group included my brother Morris. He told me of many clashes he and his comrades had with Leibrandt's anti-Semites.

The divisions between the Afrikaners and the British were felt in almost all areas of society and, to some extent, are felt even to this day. In Natal province, for example, British outlook and culture predominate. In fact, Durban was called the last outpost of the British Empire, "more British than Britain." With its colonial mentality, it was in some ways more insidiously anti-Semitic than the other Afrikaner-dominated communities in South

Africa. The Afrikaner was much more straightforward and direct in expressing his opinions than his British counterpart. The Boer Afrikaner farmer, in particular, was a much friendlier fellow than the "typical" Durbanite. In the Free State and in the countryside, one felt the unique texture of Afrikaner culture.

❖ ❖ ❖

The Boer Afrikaner can trace his ancestry in South Africa to the arrival of colonists from Holland who set up a mainland trading base for the Dutch East India Company in 1652. It was not long after the first passage to the Dark Continent was recorded that more explorers and commercial adventurers found their way to the lusciously rich southern Cape of Africa. Over the years, Europe's maritime powers fought for control of the trade routes and the natural resources of southern continental Africa. British voyagers soon followed the Dutch example and found their way to the Cape area in increasing numbers.

The British had taken over control of the Cape during the latter years of the eighteenth century and in 1820 about 5,000 British settlers landed there. Unemployment was rampant after the Napoleonic Wars and they were determined to test their luck, even if it meant travelling so far from home. The increasingly large numbers of British colonists brought with them their relatively liberal British customs and traditions of governance—freedom of the press, trial by jury, and abolition of slavery—that clashed with the outlook of the Dutch-Boer settlers, many of whom had lived in the area for generations.

A number of Dutch Afrikaners decided to escape British control and set out on the Great Trek north and east. Between 10,000 and 20,000 Afrikaners headed out in their wagons between 1834 and 1836. They were known as the Voortrekkers.

The movement of such large numbers of people through the wilderness worried the black Zulu tribes who saw the

Voortrekkers moving through their homelands. According to the history taught in South Africa when I was a schoolchild, the leader of the Trekkers, Piet Retief, and a number of his Boer companions, were interested in negotiating a treaty with Zulu chief Dingaan that would divide the Natal area between the two groups.

On February 6, 1838, Dingaan hosted a royal feast to finalize the treaty with Retief. But on Dingaan's instructions, Retief and seventy of his companions were killed. Ten months later, on December 16, the Boers took their vengeance on the Zulu at the battle of the Blood River. A force of about five hundred men led by Andries Pretorius, armed with a cannon and rifles, defeated a force of about 12,500 Zulus. More than 3,000 Zulus lost their lives; none of the Boers were killed.

That battle entered the folklore and mythology of the South African Boers and reinforced their hardened, frontier, abstemious, deeply religious, Calvinist way of life. The victory confirmed in their minds their "superiority" over the blacks and their belief that they were set on a path approved by God Himself. They were determined to set up their own republic without deference to the "modern" but naive notions they believed the British were determined to impose on them.

Tensions with the British resurfaced constantly, culminating in the Anglo-Boer wars of 1899 to 1902. Ultimately, the British won. A modus vivendi between the two cultures was enshrined in the treaties that they signed, although the Afrikaners never really forgave the British for the system of concentration camps that they had established during the wars.

Some historians record that "having lost the war, the Boers won the peace" and that the terms the British offered to the Boers to end the wars were very generous.

The British decided to grant generous terms in order to

ensure an enduring influence in southern Africa. This was largely at the expense of Africans, who were excluded from political power and forced to give back much of the land retaken from Boers during the war years. The British did not object in 1909 when the South African National Convention opted for a constitution that ensured the retention of political power in white, predominantly Afrikaner, hands.

By virtue of the newly enshrined union, Cape Town became the legislative capital of the country; Pretoria, the administrative capital; and Bloemfontein, the judicial capital. The system of governance that would ensure nearly another century of societal, political, and legal strife was thereby engraved into the stone of South African government and mores.

❖ ❖ ❖

In our fourth year of medical school, we focused on the study of pharmacology, public health, and forensic medicine. More important than the subjects that we studied in the lecture hall and laboratory, however, was the fact that we finally met our first patients. We began our clinical training in the wards, making our rounds in teams of at least six people. At the head of the team was the chief, then the assistant chief, followed by the registrar (resident), the houseman (intern), the nurses, and, finally, the students. We learned by sharing ideas, discussing problems, exchanging views, debating, comparing notes, and listening to what our chief had to say.

The chief asked the questions. The students answered them, or tried to. We were the lowest rung on the totem pole. Exchanges were always for the sake of the medical issue and in furtherance of our knowledge, but sometimes we simply got it wrong. I recall one time, just before Pesach, when we encountered a problem that seemed intractable. We must have so frustrated our chief that he threw up his hands and asked rhetorically, but poignantly, if we had matzah stuck in our ears! Over the course of the year, these were the times that, with our chief and the rest of the team, we learned how to conduct a proper examination of a patient, how to take a patient's history. The lessons stayed with me for the rest of my life.

A proper clinical examination required at least an hour. In the vast majority of cases, all the equipment I needed, I carried in my doctor's kit: stethoscope, blood-pressure instruments, vials of adrenaline, antihistamines, some bandages, a pen, and a prescription pad. We had no antibiotics yet. The sulpha drugs that we would eventually use as antibiotics were still more than two years away from coming onto the market. Occasionally, we relied upon the X-ray machine. But even the most sophisticated medical tools would be of little or no use without the best diagnostic instruments: our five senses, our wits, our judgment, and our confidence to ask as many questions as were needed to get at the problem.

In our fourth year, we also received our first introduction to the casualty department (emergency ward). Early that year, I learned to tie suture knots with one hand. An orderly taught me. In the frequent rush of the casualty department we learned a great many skills quickly.

In our last two years, we concentrated on our sub-specialties such as ear, nose, and throat, dermatology, and urology. By now we were starting to feel like the doctors we were well on our way to becoming. In school we continued with the three basic subjects of medicine: surgery, gynecology, and obstetrics. In our fifth year, we each had to perform twenty deliveries.

I quite enjoyed my six years of medical school. As I have said, I was one of the youngest in my class when I entered the hallowed halls at the age of sixteen and still was when I left—at the ripe-old age of twenty-two! Medical school forced me to grow up rather quickly. I had no choice. We were constantly tested, both by individuals and by situations and constantly judged by those same individuals, by our peers, and, perhaps, by our harshest judges—ourselves.

I was determined to be the very best physician my skills and my temperament would allow. Fortunately, by disposition, I was suited to the rigours and sometimes to the "horrors" of medicine. Forensic medicine, for example, required a bit of getting used to at first for some of my colleagues. Autopsies took a toll on the sensibilities of even veteran physicians. It was not surprising, therefore, that some less experienced initiates occasionally cringed at what they saw and did in the lab. But it did not affect me in the way it did some others.

Dealing with death was seldom a philosophical or metaphysical issue for me as much as it was a clinical inevitability. From my very first exposure to death, as I meticulously cut and picked my way through the exposed organs of a cadaver, to those inevitable moments later in my career, when I desperately tried, but failed, to arrest a cancer or to restore a critically damaged blood vessel, I set aside all but medical considerations of the task at hand. One accepted death because one marvelled at the ingenious physical structure of the human being. And it was, after all, for the sake of the human being that we strove beyond all striving to restore damaged blood vessels or to arrest a destructive cancer.

Notwithstanding my predisposition for the nature of the work, my path through medical school was greatly smoothed by very strong and loyal friendships. We were a group of six friends: Jerry Jammy, Eddie Solow, Roy Morris—whose father, the lawyer H. H. Morris had achieved great fame by defending the notorious murderer Daisey DeMelker—Sydney Sax, Gwen Greenman, and I. We were companions at study in the classroom, on the wards, and at play around the bridge tables in the common room or at the cinema. One year we all piled into a car and travelled more than 2,400 kilometres from medical school in Johannesburg to the south Cape to witness a total eclipse of the sun. After twenty-four hours, we were back at school, having travelled at over 160 kph.

Tragically, Eddie died in a gunshot accident some years later. Syd became the Secretary of Health in Australia. Roy became a specialist in internal medicine and Jerry became a good family doctor.

It was a momentous time in the world and in our lives. South Africa was at war. The Jews of Europe were being systematically hunted down and slaughtered. At the same time, the Jews of Palestine were rising up. My circle of friends joined the Zionist organization on campus to lend whatever support and assistance we could to our kinsmen and co-religionists in their respective perils so very far away.

Thus we prepared to become doctors.

"Believe me when I say that I write this letter
with deep sincerity and great appreciation
for all you did for Margaret when she was ill.
"I can't tell you what you did for her morale (and mine)
when all was not smooth. But after each visit of yours
she drew fresh strength which enabled her to see
all her difficulties through to a successful conclusion.
"What a great team you three chaps make. But all teams
must have a leader and it is not the least bit disrespectful to
your partners to say what an outstanding
surgeon/doctor/friend you are."
—S. WHITAKER, JUNE 1967

CHAPTER 5 | **Internships and marriage**

I GRADUATED IN DECEMBER 1942. Of the 150 students who started medical school, some eighty finished. I returned to Durban to begin my internship at Addington Hospital, living in residence on the grounds of the hospital, with my own bedroom but sharing dining and bathroom facilities. The woman who ran the residence looked after us very well even though there were shortages of many commodities due to the war. For example, she took the extra time to make her own white flour, which was generally unavailable in the wartime shortages, by sifting the brown flour that was distributed in abundance. With her homemade white flour, she made us scones. Her scones were so well-known that our residence was usually very busy on Sunday with guests who came specially to share tea and scones with us.

There were only ten interns at the hospital, but I was quickly made aware of my Jewishness through a de facto system of discriminatory hiring practices that reserved internship positions for the sons of the chiefs, the heads of the departments in the various wards. There was one Jewish chief at the time, the head of pediatrics, Max Kaplan. I attended his son's bris and this same son, many years later, became my auditor when I went back into practice.

My first job was in surgery, only because the chief had no son who was a doctor. In those days, internships were not compulsory after graduation, but I wanted to do them. Now, of course, they are compulsory. In addition to my internship in surgery, I also did ones in gynecology and obstetrics, pediatrics, and internal medicine.

Interns, then as now, worked very long and very hard hours. But I accepted it. We worked alternate days and alternate weekends of intake each week—intake being a period of twenty-four hours. For our labour we received £5 a month; a senior intern got £8 a month. But our accommodation was paid for. In fact, the pediatric intern was housed in his own self-contained suite, a highly prized commodity. Even though they were modest, our wages could stretch quite far. Admission to a tea-room cinema cost sixpence; a regular cinema cost 1 shilling, but we would have to sit at the back for that price. A newspaper cost tuppence; a soda pop cost a penny, as did an ice cream cone.

There was almost always a bridge game being played in the lounge and matches could easily last for up to twenty-four hours at a time. As one of us was called away from the table, another of the group took his place. We were all on call and could not go too far away from the hospital. In those internship years, bridge was also a source of income supplement. I enjoyed the game immensely. It appealed to my mathematical and systematic way of thinking. I first learned to play bridge in high school and, as I mentioned, in medical school we played regularly between lectures. Subsequently, when I lived briefly in Pretoria, I even played competitively. To this day, I still play once a week, but purely for recreation.

Part of my duties included treating the British sailors who docked in Durban. But docking in Durban was not always a certainty for those sailors because German submarines lay in wait for them, blockading them, as they steamed toward South African shores. For the first time, sharks came to the Indian Ocean waters off Durban. World War II brought them, swimming into our ocean to feed off of the corpses of the dead sailors whom the German submarines had cast into the water.

I remember a time around 2:00 on one quiet summer night

when a sailor came in to the hospital after a heavy bout of drinking. He was uncontrollably violent. The sisters on duty couldn't calm him, nor could the orderlies. I was called into the emergency room and we put that sailor into a straitjacket to let him "sleep it off." Meanwhile, I went to bed and fell asleep. After a period of time, I was awoken by a call that the sailor was crying from the pain and discomfort of his restraints. I let him sit in it for another hour before I made my way down to him. That was the only time I ever used a straitjacket.

Because there was still no medical school in Durban, the senior staff of the hospital were all part-timers whose primary work was in their private practices. One senior consultant, one junior consultant, and an intern looked after two wards, male and female, comprising forty to fifty beds. There were no registrars, thus the intern assumed a great deal of responsibility, indeed much more than he or she would today. After two to three months, I could operate on an acute appendicitis.

After my internship year, I stayed on for an additional year as the senior intern at Addington. I ran the casualty ward, did six months of anesthetics, and most of the surgery that the chiefs did not want to do or that the interns could not do. During this time I carried out procedures that would normally have been performed by the junior consultant. This allowed me to hone and refine my skills to a degree not generally done at comparable career stages, then or today.

House calls comprised a large portion of my practice. I made up to twenty a day when I worked in Pretoria and when I was on my various locums in Durban. This meant starting the day very early and finishing very late. I also had to respond to frequent nighttime emergency calls. By the time I finished that second year I could take out an appendix, fix a hernia, tap a chest, open an abdomen, even open a skull by myself. From the very beginning, I was deft with my fingers and quick with my surgery, which was very important for the patient since we had no antibiotics at that time. Finishing surgery as quickly as possible was important to minimizing the chance of infection setting in.

I remember the very first time I cut open an abdomen. I was tentative. I was reluctant to press hard enough. I made three or four strokes before I managed to cut through the fat. And then I touched the muscle area. Later, with a bit more experience, I was able to cut through all the layers in one stroke.

When I started in surgery, anesthetics were rather primitive. We used a rag, a bottle, a mask, and a bit of flannel over the mask on which we poured ether. But in Durban, we could not get the patient to sleep with ether alone. It was too hot. The ether evaporated too rapidly. Thus, we used ethyl chloride, a substance that, when squirted onto the mask, would put a patient to sleep in thirty or forty seconds. But often, a patient going under from that could become violent as well. Once he was "under" we would start pouring our ether on quickly and if that was not enough we used chloroform. Eventually, we became quite proficient in using a chloroform–ether mixture. Some of us would use pure chloroform. But chloroform could only be applied drop by drop because it was a cardiac poison. If one applied too much chloroform, the patient could die.

When the patient was asleep, we would connect him to oxygen with a mask. We had endotracheal tubes that we could put down the windpipe but we had to be very careful and skillful. Pentothal was introduced in 1944 or 1945, as was evipan, both of which were given intravenously to put a patient to sleep.

The year went by very quickly because I was so very busy. Life was busy; life was hectic; life was full—but it was not so busy or hectic or full that it warranted complaint. I knew that as an intern, I would occasionally have to work twenty-four hours a day. But fatigue and exhaustion were no excuse. When the chief came to the ward for rounds at 8:00 a.m., I had to be there promptly.

After my senior year, I knew I was going to specialize.

Treatment in the hospitals in South Africa was completely free to patients, although, of course, patients were segregated into different hospitals according to the colour of their skin. King Edward VIII Hospital served black patients. Coloureds—according to South African law, these were individuals who were the products of the union of whites and blacks—were treated in a specific wing of Addington Hospital. We treated all patients the same, regardless of colour, but the conditions under which white and black patients lived—economic, educational, housing, social, communal, nutritional—were so vastly different. Even the diseases, I would discover over the years, were different.

Indians, of whom there were a significant number in Durban especially, had their own private hospital called St. Aidan's. In 1945, however, there were no full-time doctors on the hospital payroll. One physician, employed part-time, was the hospital's functional full-time staff. The rest of the doctors who worked at St. Aidan's were in private practice. There were some Indian doctors at this time, although only a few. As they were not yet allowed to train in the medical schools in South Africa, they were forced to train elsewhere, often overseas. In fact, many received their medical training in Dublin.

Nor would any medical school in South Africa accept blacks at this time. It would be some years still before the doors of medical school opened to them.

Perhaps as a concession to some shred of conscience, however, or more likely, simply as an act of self-interested expedience, the government did allow coloureds to go to medical school. A number did, especially in Cape Town, where a large portion of the coloured community lived.

My family was doing well at this time. My parents were in good health. Morris had gone into business, running an automobile repair garage, my father having managed to arrange for the licence through his political connections. Hymie was twenty and also opened his own business, selling and supplying stationery. Havis was fifteen and still at school.

The war was coming to an end; soldiers were being released from active duty. At home, at work, in our clubs, in various other social settings and groups, my family and friends spoke about the situation of the Jews in Europe. In addition to the news we received from the regular newspaper and radio sources, we also received information from the Durban Jewish Club.

Having completed two years at Addington Hospital and a three-week locum for a doctor in Durban, in January 1945, I went to Pretoria to do a year of family practice. The group of doctors with whom I worked in Pretoria was Epstein, Klein, and Immerman. Epstein eventually became a pediatrician and moved to England; Klein stayed on in Pretoria; Immerman became an ear, nose, and throat specialist and today lives in Atlanta.

Our patients were both black and white and I learned a great deal because of the wide variety of medicine the practice encompassed. I was often called by the police to tend to a medical situation in the townships. In those days there were very few, if any, telephones in the homes of the blacks who lived outside the city. They therefore went to a nearby police station to call for a doctor. Blacks worked in the city but did not live there—except for the women, that is. The black women lived in shacks in the backyards of their white employers, separated from their families, even their husbands and children, who lived in the townships.

Gynecology and obstetrics was a large part of the Pretoria practice; we often were called to the most interesting situations to do deliveries. I often went out in the middle of the night to Atteridgeville, Bantule, and Eersterus—the black townships—to help a patient deliver her baby on the floor of a mud hut. Sometimes I had to walk as much as a kilometre in the pitch black of night. But I felt no fear; there was no sense of danger then.

Toward the end of 1945, I decided to specialize as a surgeon.

I also decided to marry a beautiful young woman named Lola Jankelson. Even before we were married, Lola often went with me on these house calls and she would wait for me alone in the car. Neither she nor I ever worried for her safety.

I had met Lola in Durban the year before and was actually introduced to her, ironically, by a girlfriend at the time. Lola was a pharmacy student, the only woman in her class. One year later, in Pretoria, I decided to renew my acquaintance with her. That acquaintanceship progressed to the point where I fell in love with her. Lola's sister, Annette, was already engaged to Max Melmed and planning a wedding for October 14. I suggested we do the same: get married and plan our wedding for the very same day as her sister. Thankfully, she must have thought it was a good idea because she agreed.

Lola's mother did all the catering for both weddings, which were held at Wolmarans Street Shul, the large main shul in Johannesburg. The reception was at the Stephanie Hotel, which Lola's parents owned and operated.

Lola and I came from different Jewish backgrounds. My parents' home was an observant one; Lola's parents' home was not. But the Steins lived in Durban and the Jankelsons, Moey and

Freda, lived in Johannesburg. They therefore got on well with each other. The distance between their respective homes ensured that no incident ever occurred to diminish their mutual respect for each other.

Lola's mother was born in South Africa, in Oudtshoorn, the area famous for its ostrich farms. Lola's father came to South Africa from Riga, Latvia, although he was born in Zagor in Lithuania.

Lola's father, a quiet, gentle, cultured, and scholarly man, was another example of the steel-hard determination that motivated so many of his generation. Though his formal education stopped at the age of twelve when he came, alone, to South Africa, his self-education was on a wide scale, extending to intellectual and cultural curiosities that were very rare for the time and place. Although the family lived modestly, he managed to collect a good number of records, thereby enabling him to learn the corpus of classical and new operas; indeed, he could identify all the major arias from the Italian, French, and German classics. My father-in-law was also a superb chess player. A number of chessboards were always set up in the various corners of his study and he carried on simultaneous matches through correspondences with opponents around the world. He also spoke a number of languages, all of which, except for his mother tongue, Yiddish, he taught himself. He died in 1969.

Lola's mother died in 1995 at the age of ninety-four. Until she was ninety, she was in good health and still doing petit-point needlework and crocheting. Then, she fractured her hip and was somehow never able to recover from the injury. She deteriorated quite quickly after that mishap.

But there was no doubt about the impact that the quiet, cultured, loving atmosphere of the Jankelson home exerted on the personalities of their children. For never in my life had I ever encountered anyone as cheerful, positive, soft-spoken, and simply delightful as Lola. She was a woman of extreme delicacy and grace.

Once Lola and I were married, we moved to Durban. My father was friendly with the mayor, Sidney Smith. It was a friendship that was remarkable in its own right. My father had moved to Durban in mid-life from the darker climes of Lithuania, already set in his eastern-European ways. Yet he very quickly mastered the languages and the nuances of his new home and developed long-lasting friendships with members of the political elite. I often marvelled at my father's unique social and, dare I say, political, skills. He did not anglicize his name. He remained, always, Yudel. Nor did he compromise his religious beliefs. No one tried to telephone him on Shabbat because they knew he would not answer the phone. How was he able, so quickly, so easily, to find his way around City Hall? I do not know. On a number of occasions, my father's friendship with the mayor would prove helpful to Lola and me. For example, on our return to Durban by train, we were met at the station by the mayor's driver and car, in which we were properly transported to my parents' home there. We were greeted with a festive little party that my mother made for us.

Thus, I brought my bride of one month into the family home in Durban. We displaced Morris, who now had to share a bedroom with Havis. No one in my family expected Lola to help out in the kitchen; my mother would never have let her in any event. After we settled in, we went on a two-week honeymoon in Scottburgh on the south coast of Natal.

It was at this stage in our lives that we began to think more about the morality and propriety of having our black domestic staff living in our backyard. As I have already mentioned, domestic help lived alone in a shack at the back of the house, without husband or children. The law did not allow them to live together. What were the servants really thinking? Didn't they miss their families? Perhaps it was because we ourselves were newlyweds and, as a result, more aware of the blessing, companionship, and significance of married life, that the issues seemed so much starker to us. When we were younger and children ourselves, such questions never dawned on us. It was different for our children who grew up in a far more enlightened and turbulent social milieu and in a home where the issues of apartheid were constantly discussed. They did not accept the surrealistic routine of everyday South African life in the way that we had.

Although it is neither a defence nor a justification of the way we lived our lives, Jewish people, on balance, treated their servants better than the majority of the white population of South Africa did. We were more concerned for our servants' standard of living, as it were. Thus, we and most of our friends tried to ensure that our servants had proper personal and household amenities and facilities that protected, at least to that extent, their fundamental inherent dignity.

I do not recall the questions surrounding apartheid being discussed in synagogue pulpits when I was young. This was a reflection of the relative docility of the community. Later on, however, as times changed and after Rabbis Rabinowitz, Caspar, Weiss, and Cyril Harris came to Johannesburg, the morality of the apartheid structure found its way onto the community's social and political agenda. We knew even after the war, although perhaps we did not discuss it enough among our friends, that the treatment of the blacks was creating a pressure-cooker existence from which a social explosion was inevitable, merely a matter of time. In a few years, British Prime Minister Harold Macmillan would warn South Africans about "the winds of change" blowing across our continent. Those winds would ultimately bring a storm.

But this would come much later. When Lola and I were still newlyweds, married for less than three months, we decided to go to Edinburgh where I would do my fellowship in surgery and then some postgraduate training in London. Lola had finished her pharmaceutical training. And it seemed like the right moment to set off for Europe. My plan had always been to specialize in surgery, but to get onto the specialist's register I had to do two years of family practice. I had already completed one qualifying year in Pretoria as well as a few months of substitute locums for other doctors, but I still needed six more months to qualify for the register.

By the time we left for Europe, I had already administered some 1,500 anesthetics of which two hundred were spinal anesthetics. The experience would serve me well in obtaining one of the diplomas I sought in Europe, a qualification in anesthesiology.

"If anyone was sick in our household—beyond flu—
no treatment would be commenced without a prior consultation
with Mannie. Thirty years ago my late father broke his hip.
Unfortunately the broken hip resulted in his being ill for over two
years. At times his problems were even life threatening. Mannie
was there almost on a daily basis,
sometimes dressing wounds or just talking to him and
giving him and the family encouragement.
"When my mother fell ill, her problems went from bad to worse,
resulting in her losing a leg and eventually dying from
her complicated conditions. Mannie, once again was in and out of
the family home—for years—sometimes on a daily basis,
but often more than once a day. His warmth, wisdom, and understanding were of great comfort to my mother who,
most of the time, was saddened and depressed due to
her deteriorating condition…
"Mannie was not only a brilliant doctor and surgeon, who gave
of his advice, but he understood how encouraging the sick patient
was so vitally important. He took time off from his busy practice
to look after friends, and even when he was not treating them, he
gave them moral support and encouragement…An account never
appeared for the hours that he spent in our home.
His kindness to my family was repeated with other families, too.
Not only did he care for his friends, but it was also told by
patients who did not have the means to pay, that Mannie would
operate at reduced fees and even without charging.
"His moving away from Durban was
an enormous loss for the community."
—JONATHAN BEARE, APRIL 2001

| **Postgraduate studies overseas**

W E MANAGED TO FIND PASSAGE to England in January 1946. This was a great feat, as any means of transport beyond the borders of the country was difficult to find, and if one did find extra-territorial passage, it came at a high premium. Priority was given to women and children who had been evacuated during the war from the UK to South Africa and to returning soldiers.

Air travel was then in its infancy; travelling by amphibious plane from South Africa was a long and tedious affair. The plane touched down at several different lakes on the continent on its journey northward. It took four days to get to the UK.

Ever resourceful, my father secured accommodation for Lola and me on a transport ship to England with the aid of his good friend, Sidney Smith, the mayor of Durban, who was by then also a member of the South African Senate.

My father had always been kind to Smith. That was why he was always so friendly to our family. Smith had left school at the age of fourteen and was forced to fend for himself from an early age. When Smith needed a place for the night, father let him sleep in the lounge of our home. But Smith had a natural intelligence and a driving curiosity. His lack of formal schooling was not an impediment; he was self-taught and eventually rose to great heights and positions of responsibility by sheer force of will and determination.

The heart-pounding excitement Lola and I felt when we climbed aboard ship quickly vanished like raindrops in the ocean in discomfort, disappointment, and frustration. I was given a bunk in a hammock in the hold five levels below sea level. Lola, my young bride of three months, shared a two-berth cabin with five other women many levels above the hold in which I "holed" up. Each day I had to line up with a tin plate and cup to collect food. But as I was seasick most of the time I did not eat very much anyway. I had a terrible time of it. Most of the days I spent on deck where I could be with Lola and breathe fresh air—that is, when the ship was not yawing to and fro, side to side, back and forth through the heaving waves. After fourteen days of this newlywed and gastro-intestinal hell, we landed, at long last, in Southampton and took a train to London where we settled into a hotel. It was winter in the UK and very cold.

There were numerous lectures and tutorials at all of the many London teaching hospitals in this postwar era. As a result, postgraduate students from all over the world were here, availing themselves of this opportunity to advance their medical studies. The hospitals themselves were quite dilapidated. There was nothing modern about them—the stairs were rickety and the halls uniformly drab. But the teaching and the professors were excellent.

I attended the postgraduate medical school in Hammersmith Hospital. Here I had the unique experience of giving an anesthetic for the great Professor Grey Turner. I must have been a bit too eager because he told his students and the other doctors in the theatre, "We wait until the anesthetist says we can start and only then do we start."

Anesthesia was always a problem for field hospitals, especially in hot-climate countries, but the war had spawned significant advances in the field. Nonetheless there were still complications. The method at that time was by an injection of pentothal or a mask over the face with nitrous oxygen and ether. Unfortunately, if one used ether, one could not use a diathermy to stop bleeding—diathermy coagulates bleeding by producing an electric current—because, when combined with the ether, it might cause an explosion.

Turner was the first person to reconstruct an artificial esophagus (gullet). He joined the throat to the stomach by placing a segment of large bowel with its blood supply intact in front of the breastbone. At that time, the chest cavity could not be opened because there was no means of keeping the lungs inflated. No cuffed tracheal tubes had yet been devised. Turner's invention set the stage for the repair and replacement of the gullet, which was often destroyed by acids, thus enabling a person to swallow again. He was one of the great names in surgery.

The ability to safely open the chest during surgery came only in the early 1940s. Before then, one could not perform heart or lung surgery. The only lung surgery that was attempted was for tuberculosis sufferers whose lungs had been destroyed. In that case, we would perform a thoracoplasty. We would not open the chest, but would take out the ribs and allow the chest to fall in to compress the lung in an attempt to induce healing, which never happened. It was the development of Henry Boyle's apparatus and the resulting closed-circuit anesthesia that made open-chest surgery possible. The patient breathed in and out of a tube with a cuff blown up at the lower end of the tube; no air or anesthetic gas could escape.

In London I studied at Hammersmith, St. Mary's Hospital, and the Children's' Hospital at Great Ormond Street. It was an exciting time. We heard lectures on a variety of subjects from some of the leading medical scholars of our time, who would present case histories and then discuss them with us.

After some months in London, Lola and I went to Edinburgh where I enrolled in a postgraduate course at the Royal Infirmary of Edinburgh. To begin with, we found accommodation in a small residential hotel.

That winter of 1946 was one of the coldest winters on record in Scotland. Coming from Durban, Lola and I experienced what I can only call climatic shock. Edinburgh's thermometer seemed stuck at -15° Celsius (rather than Durban's usual low of +15° Celsius) for most of the entire year we spent there. In the evenings, we would huddle and shiver in our one room with our coats on, trying to keep warm. The room had a small gas heater that we constantly fed with shillings to provide us some extra measure of warmth. We were always cold.

Lola's pharmaceutical degree was recognized in the UK and she was thus able to find work at Baildon's Pharmacy on Princess Street near Edinburgh's famous castle. She earned the princely sum of £30 per month, but this was enough to support our meagre needs. She would walk, or rather slip, slide, and sometimes slosh in the snow to work a kilometre away.

I, on the other hand, attended lectures at the Royal Infirmary's magisterial great hall with its high ceilings, wood-panelled walls and stone floor—but no central heating. We sat hunched over in our seats, in full overcoats and scarves, trying to keep warm and take notes at the same time. The lectures were informative and, at times, even stimulating, but keeping my fingers warm was as much of a challenge as deciphering the notes my frozen digits scrawled onto the pages of my workbook. After lectures, even on Sundays, I went to the Infirmary to take part in ward rounds with residents, interns, and postgraduates.

Edinburgh was well-known as an excellent place for learning medicine. Here I came across all the great names I had heard of and read about during my undergraduate training and from whose textbooks I had studied. For example, there was Mercer, Quarry-Wood, and Learmonth, who was also a son-in-law of one of the Mayos of the famous Mayo clinic. I was able to get to know some of the junior lecturers fairly well. In later years, this stood me in good stead when Lola and I returned to the UK. By that time, they had all become successful professors and heads of departments at various hospitals and other key institutions in London. Ian Aird became professor at the postgraduate school at Hammersmith in London; John Wilkinson became head of the Children's Hospital in London; and John Bruce became professor at Edinburgh University.

What an opportunity it was for me to learn. I wanted to soak up as much knowledge and gain as much hands-on experience as I could in the time that I knew would pass all too quickly.

Lola and I spent the evenings warding off the damp cold that permeated our hotel room and comparing notes of the day. In her pharmacy, Lola learned first-hand how the Scots got the reputation for being "canny." She told one story of an old man who came into the shop one day asking for a bottle with a rubber stopper rather than the usual cork. His reason? The cork stopper, he pointed out to Lola, would absorb some of the medicine that he was paying for. Another time, she recounted the tale of a man who came into the pharmacy and pointed out to her that his bottle of saccharine had contained only ninety-eight tablets instead of the one hundred promised on the label. But he was not complaining, he explained, since his previous bottle had contained 103 tablets. It's interesting to note that such amusingly trivial and harmless incidents can evoke such memories more than a half century later. The Scots were indeed industrious, hard-working, and very friendly to us.

These were difficult days for the Scots. They were still feeling the aftermath of the war. Food and even clothing were rationed more strictly than they had been during the war. We were each allowed one fresh egg and two ounces of fat per week. There was very little meat to be had and thus very little meat in our diet. We lived mainly on bread, potatoes, and

Brussels sprouts. To this very day, I do not and will not eat Brussels sprouts. I had my fill of them some fifty-five years ago. After a while we found more comfortable lodgings in a country house whose owner, having fallen on hard times, called us her "paying guests."

Both sets of parents sent us food parcels containing sealed butter tins, chocolates, candy, meat, condensed milk, and other delicacies. We shared our bounty with some of the many South Africans who were also studying in Edinburgh and who were part of our circle of acquaintances. One of my South African postgraduate colleagues was Goff Charlewood. He would eventually become a senior gynecologist in Johannesburg and deliver our son, Mike, during my stint as a teacher at the medical school there. Charlewood was regarded as one of the best; he had exceptional technical skills.

Some of my professors made a point of inviting us to their homes. It was on these occasions that Lola and I had our first taste of such traditional Scottish cuisine as black pudding, haggis, and rabbit. Times were indeed difficult.

While we were in Edinburgh, Lola's father won £1,000 on a ticket in the Rhodesian lottery. As was his nature, he generously split the prize among his three daughters. With Lola's share we bought a Morris Minor and were thus able to travel throughout the Scottish highlands and villages and see much of the country. We drove up the west coast to Inverness, down the east coast, and back to Edinburgh. We stayed a night at the old Trossacks Castle and went to Loch Ness. It was exciting and a great deal of fun.

Early in 1947, at the age of twenty-six, I obtained my fellowship in surgery—one of the youngest, if not the youngest, in the group to do so. Although my parents had taught me not to submit too often or too deeply to feelings of vanity and self-congratulations, I could not help but feel a combination of pride at my achievement and gratitude for the opportunity that was now drawing to a close.

We left Edinburgh in our black Morris Minor and headed to London. Once in London, we sold the car because, in truth, it was no longer necessary. We were happy to rely on London's well-developed, sophisticated transport system. We even managed to sell the Minor for more than we had paid for it!

London was a mixed blessing for Lola and me. The effects of the war were evident everywhere. Living conditions were still quite harsh. Food and other staples were in short supply. As an indication of the austerity of the times, restaurants in London could only offer a two-course meal, for a shilling. If one wanted to eat more than the two courses, one had to hop from one table to another or from one restaurant to another. The government of Winston Churchill had been thrown out of power. People were palpably weary from the nightmarish trauma of the war. Rebuilding the city was their first priority.

Despite the strained economic and social conditions, I was still able to further my medical studies. I found a locum in family medicine in Dover for three weeks, a typical country practice in which we lived in the doctor's house. Life was much easier for us there than it had been in London. As partial payment for our services, many of the farmers brought us eggs, which we had not seen for some eighteen months. Our stay in London, though, was certainly not all hardship and study. We also travelled extensively around England, getting to know the country as well as we had Scotland. We explored a great deal of Middlesex County, the lakes area, and the seaside resorts. It was a truly wonderful time in our lives.

Lola's sister, Adeline, and a friend, Doreen Harrison, came from South Africa to visit us. We decided to cross the channel to explore the continent. We arranged a tour of Switzerland, France, and Italy. Europe was still in a state of postwar shambles with no real currency controls. We travelled for five weeks and did not spend more than £100. Swiss banks would exchange a £1 British traveller's cheque for 17 Swiss francs. At a different counter at the same bank, one could then buy a British pound note for 9 Swiss francs. We took advantage of the differential and, in this way, bought Italian lira and French francs.

After Adeline and her friend returned to South Africa, Lola and I decided to travel from Liverpool to Dublin—by boat. I must not have remembered the shipboard experience a year earlier on our journey to the UK. Although the distance between Liverpool and Dublin was not great, the discomfort and physical distress on that voyage was. There could not have been a rougher crossing. My poor nerves, my poor stomach.

The earliest passage we could arrange back to South Africa from London was not until sometime in 1948. Thus I went up to the Nuffield Institute in Oxford to do a short course in anesthesia. I was accepted for the course because I had been a resident in anesthesia for six months in Durban. My mentors were Mackintosh and Mushin, who, at that time, were already working on closed-circuit anesthesia. They perfected the endotracheal tube that facilitated chest surgery. The tube went into the lung; the other end of the tube had a cuff. The tube was connected to a machine from which various gases were pumped through the tube into the lung. The gases were absorbed by a filtering substance and then returned back up into the machine. This system permitted surgery inside the chest, since one could inflate the lungs with positive pressure.

In August 1947 we left London for Dublin, where we intended to stay until it was time to return home. I signed onto a course in gynecology and obstetrics at the Rotunda Hospital of Trinity University of Dublin. Much to my chagrin, spouses of the postgraduate students were not permitted to live at the hospital, even though undergraduate female students from out of town were. As a result, Lola had to stay at a nearby hotel while I lived in the Rotunda Hospital. However I did manage to smuggle Lola into the residence to spend the occasional night with me. Of course that also meant that I had to smuggle her out of the residence before dawn, which I always did successfully and with a great deal of satisfaction.

At that time Rotunda Hospital was known as one of the leading maternity hospitals in the world and it attracted postgraduate students from all over. We dealt exclusively with abnormal, high-risk deliveries. Babies were kept in cots with their mothers, sleeping in their mothers' beds. Today, there appears to be a return to this approach of pediatric care. We also visited patients in their homes whenever the deliveries had been problematic or fraught with complications.

Among the more interesting "medical" practices at Rotunda were the daily evening rounds of another sort with the master and the assistant master at Mooney's, the local pub, across the road from the hospital. This was apparently a Rotunda ritual. Medicine was occasionally discussed at the table, too! To this day I have kept up the taste for Guiness.

I received my Diploma in Gynecology and Obstetrics (DGO) from Trinity University, standing first in the class, after passing practical, oral, and written examinations. I also received permission to write the exam for the Diploma in Anesthesia as I had not had enough time to do so when we were in Oxford. I wrote that exam, passed, and received my second diploma from Trinity.

Our time in the UK was eye-opening and humbling. In London, the evidence of war was ubiquitous. We saw devastation everywhere in the city. Even when I returned to London in 1959, the city was still in the midst of its rebuilding and cleanup from the war.

As Ireland had not officially joined in the war, Dublin was spared the devastation that befell London and Dubliners had not experienced rationing of any kind. How enjoyable it was for us to be able to get a decent steak again, or to be able to find articles of clothing that we needed. We had a wonderful six-month stay in Dublin.

I could have stayed longer in the UK to obtain my membership in the British College of Physicians and Surgeons as well as my fellowship. I enjoyed the atmosphere, challenges, congeniality, and collegiality. But Lola felt it was time to go back home and I agreed with her.

Even with my surgery fellowship in hand, I was not certain I would actually concentrate my work in surgery. It was quite difficult to find a residency in surgery in South Africa. Due to the decommissioning of officers and the return of soldiers after the war, there were a great many people looking for similar residency postings. Thus, I applied for as many residencies as I could in Durban and eventually accepted the first one that came up. It was in surgery.

It was now time to return to South Africa. In the spring of 1948, we set sail from Southampton harbour on the luxury oceangoing Windsor Castle. I had some trepidation about embarking once again on a large boat. My previous adult experiences had proven that I was not a staunch sailor. This time, however, Lola and I at least had a two-berth cabin to ourselves. My stomach was far more settled, although still not perfect, than it had been on the trip that brought us to the UK. But this time we could readily walk about the deck and breathe the fresh air that assisted me considerably in coping with challenges to my inner ear balance and to my stomach.

We stopped at Madeira in Portugal, where Lola and I bought an embroidered, lace tablecloth that we used on special family and holiday occasions for the rest of our lives. In a very concrete and tangible way, the memory of that happy time in our young married lives was woven into countless other warm memories that were spun from the joyous, festive moments around our family table. That tablecloth is still in very good condition.

We had fun on the way home. The organizers of the voyage made certain to provide a variety of entertainment on board, including dances, games, and various athletic activities. At one costume ball, I dressed as Gandhi. As I was quite thin at that time, the Gandhi appearance was an easy one to replicate dressed in a white sheet and with a face painted in cocoa. The costume was sufficiently original and the likeness was sufficiently striking to garner a third-place prize. First prize went to a man who dressed, quite uniquely, as "The Last Drop (in the Bottle)."

Lola and I were very happy. It was 1948.

*"I have no desire to spill my emotions like ink, but, Sir,
I feel I simply must write to you and tell you how much
my wife and I feel indebted to you.
"Uppermost in our minds is relief from a burdening anxiety and
deep appreciation of your care, attention, and unfailing courtesy,
and lastly, great admiration of your skill. May God guide that
skill of your hand for a long, long time
for the benefit of sick mankind.
"I hope this does not appear too maudlin and mushy;
I have never really been more sincere in my life."*
—J. B. SHEEHAN, MARCH 1962

| **Return to Durban**

M Y PARENTS AND BROTHERS met us at the port in Durban. We arrived home with the happy news that Lola was pregnant. Our parents were thrilled, as were we. It was time now to embark on the next phase of our lives.

Because of the influx of people into the city after the war, accommodation was at a premium. So, at first, we stayed at my parents' house, although later we managed to get an apartment on the beachfront. The apartment was not far from Addington Hospital, where I had received an appointment as the first full-time registrar in surgery and was placed in charge of the casualty department. To qualify for the Surgeon's Specialists' Register in South Africa at that time, one needed to have completed one year of internship, one year as a Senior Medical Officer, two years of general practice, and three years of residency in surgery. It was a rigorous process, but I was close to qualifying. My appointment at Addington, I hoped, would soon lead to my entry into the Specialists' Register as a surgeon—a Mister.

In Britain, and in South Africa, a fellowship in surgery brought with it the title of "Mister." Misters (of surgery) did not want to be known as doctors. The differentiation dates back to the days when doctors would not accept surgeons, who had their own professional societies, as part of the medical profession. The individuals who started surgery in earlier times in Britain were considered a bit unsavoury by the doctors, or physicians. Surgeons had their beginnings in barbering and were known to steal bodies from graves to perform dissections. As a result, the doctors looked down on the "descendants" of the barbers—the surgeons. As time wore on, the surgeons responded to the doctors' stinging snub by referring to themselves as misters. Thus, the two medical groupings were differentiated. Misters did not want to be called doctors and that was fine with the doctors. Over time, as the practice of medicine modernized, the distinctions between mister and doctor gradually dissolved.

I was prepared to work very hard...and I did.

Addington had three surgical wards, and each ward was divided into male and female sections. Each ward had a chief, an assistant chief, a registrar—in this case, me—and an intern. In fact, I was the registrar for all three surgical wards. I was the only senior full-time physician on staff. The part-timers were not very keen to go out at night for emergencies and, as they thought I could handle most emergencies, they left me to deal with the many diverse crises that walked or were wheeled into the hospital. As time went on, I was left to do more and more major procedures on my own. It was an excellent way to push my skills and my self-confidence forward.

On many occasions, for example, I or the interns had to administer the anesthesia because there were no full-time anesthetists. We were still using chloroform and ether, as well as Boyle's machine and pentothal. If we did not need a muscle relaxant, we might use a continuous drip of pentothal. Today that would be frowned upon as too dangerous. In later years, we used a variety of muscle relaxants such as curare and scolene. The "curare effect" actually paralyzed the muscle, which, in itself, could pose problems. One had to be certain, when operating, that the patient was fully asleep, otherwise he or she could become paralyzed while still awake. If this should occur, the patient would then be aware of, if not actually feeling, all of the aspects of the surgery!

A great deal of surgery was performed on patients who were only under a local anesthetic. For example, I operated on thyroids that way. If I got near the nerve that runs to the vocal chord, I asked the patient to sing a high note that required full use of the vocal chord to prove that I had not cut the nerve. After a while, when we removed the thyroid gland, I was able to visually identify the nerve and work around it. Iodine insufficiencies commonly led to enlarged nodules on the thyroid, which created severe cosmetic and other medical issues for the patient. A cancerous thyroid presented different, more delicate, surgical challenges.

At Addington, I performed all types and manner of surgery. One incident I vividly recall involved the young daughter of the secretary of the medical association in Durban. The child had been brought into the hospital suffering from diphtheria. For some reason, there was quite a bit of diphtheria at that time. I was in the ward when the child arrived. She could not breathe; the disease had clogged up her throat. Right in the ward, I performed a tracheotomy, putting a tube into the child's throat so that she could breathe. Once her airway had been restored, we could then begin to treat the illness. The child fully recovered.

Another unusual incident from those days involved a patient suffering from an inflamed appendix. The appendix is a puzzling organ. We are still not sure what its function is; it appears to be a remnant of human evolutionary development. The small bowel comes into the cecum and the appendix is a little string-like thing that comes off the cecum. But because there is a lot of lymph tissue in the appendix, the pain can be quite severe when it becomes inflamed or infected. Generally speaking, there are two kinds of appendix problems: an inflammation emanating either from the bowel or from the blood that settles in the appendix, or an inflammation caused by a blockage of the opening into the appendix.

One day the doorman at the Edward Hotel, the best hotel in Durban at that time, came to the hospital. He was in some distress, suffering severe pain in his lower abdomen. I examined him and I told him his appendix had to be removed. The man looked at me rather quizzically and said his appendix had been removed some years ago in Russia. He had the scar to prove it.

I stood firm, however, and insisted that he was suffering acute appendix pain. The symptoms were unmistakable: nausea, vomiting, and pain shifts. The appendix had to come out, I told him. I was adamant. He agreed to surgery, although he was skeptical of my contention that the organ causing his pain was, in fact, his appendix.

The patient was wheeled into the operating theatre. I opened his abdomen. Sure enough! Staring back at me from was an acutely inflamed appendix. The Russian doctors had indeed operated on him, but they had left a sizable stump of the appendix intact. Over time that stump had served as a mini-appendix and became inflamed as if it were whole. The appropriate procedure for the original surgeon would have been to take out as much of the appendix as he possibly could and bury the stump inward so that whatever was left would break off into the bowel and ultimately disappear.

Most of the night work was left to me. During the days, I would come along to join the operating slates. There were six operating sessions always going on during the day.

But imagine the situation in summer! There was no air conditioning. In the deep, humid heat of the hottest days of the summer, the windows were open, the fans were constantly turning and blowing cooler but still-hot breezes on us. How sterile could it have been? And yet, sterility never seemed to be a problem. In retrospect, one must conclude that there was, indeed, more infection at that time. But it was not an obvious problem then, nor did it lead to untoward complications.

I spent almost two years this way at Addington, until the end of 1949, gaining invaluable experience in a great many aspects of surgery. But those two years only counted as one year toward my specialty certification. I still needed to complete two more years of surgical registrarship at a teaching hospital and Addington Hospital, unfortunately, was not a teaching hospital. Nor was there yet a medical school in Durban.

On October 21, 1948, our daughter, Linda, was born. The head of the obstetrics department of Addington Hospital delivered her. For the longest time, she presented as a breech birth, but he managed to turn her and she was delivered normally. I did not participate in Linda's birth. Nor was I even in the delivery room. Unlike today, fathers were not then part of the birthing process. They were not allowed into the delivery rooms. It just wasn't done, although I "hung around" close by. My mother and Lola's mother, of course, hung around with me.

By this time, Lola and I were living on our own in the small beachfront apartment. The apartment was quaint, with a view of the ocean, located, as I have said, near the hospital. It was also opposite the Durban Jewish Club—our community centre— which had tennis courts, bowling greens, a gymnasium, a bar, and a dance floor. The Jews of Durban and the Club assisted in the integration of some of the Jewish Polish soldiers who had wandered into South Africa during the war and decided to stay on afterward. Some of the soldiers stayed with us until they could get settled elsewhere.

To climb the next rung of qualification for my specialty certificate, I took up a position as registrar at the Johannesburg General Hospital and as a lecturer at the medical school of the

University of Witwatersrand. This meant that we had to move to Johannesburg. So, we drove up to Johannesburg where, with a few pieces of furniture, we set up home in a flat in Hillbrow, not far from the hotel that Lola's parents' owned. It was 1950.

In conjunction with my duties at the General Hospital, I also worked at Coronation Hospital, the teaching hospital for black patients affiliated with University of Witwatersrand. That is where I encountered the poor man who had the knife blade embedded in his skull.

There was another occasion at Coronation Hospital when circumstances required that I "raise a flap" into a patient's skull. A woman was making a nuisance of herself wandering through the casualty department and screaming. On several occasions, over a period of a month, she had been complaining very loudly of headaches. The casualty officer on call could find nothing clinically wrong with her and he considered her to be some-what of a behavioural problem.

On examination, however, it became quickly apparent that there was more to the patient's condition than the misdiagnosis of an irritated and frustrated casualty officer. I admitted her to our ward and performed a lumbar puncture. (CT scans were not yet available.) I found traces of old blood there. An X-ray of the skull showed a small fracture. The diagnosis was then obvi-ous: this poor suffering woman had a blood clot over one side of her brain. I opened her skull by raising a flap of bone and evacuated the clot. Within days, she was better.

The casualty department at Coronation Hospital provided a rich medical education for an aspiring young surgeon. Most of the cases we saw were trauma cases. We treated relatively few gastric ulcers, gall bladders, or ulcers. We did, however, treat many patients for iodine-deficient thyroid conditions. I was able to publish a number of articles about the experiences and cases that presented themselves to our staff.

For example, I reported on some 1,200 stab wounds of the chest that we saw in the casualty ward. If the patient's breathing was not too distressed—if the trachea was still in its normal place, if there was relatively little internal bleeding, even though, in some cases, the X-ray might indicate otherwise—we treated the condition in a conservative manner. The sheer number of cases we saw compelled us to do this. We would not drain the fluid. We would not put a needle into the patient's chest, for if we did, we might introduce infection. We did not intervene. We put the patients on a regime of physiotherapy, of deep breathing exercises. Three weeks later, when we reassessed them, their lungs were invariably clear. The blood from the stabbing had been re-absorbed. That was a tremendous step forward in the treatment of stab wounds to the chest because every textbook to that point called for the chest to be opened and the blood to be drained out.

Thus, we learned when and which chests to open. The incision was usually down the side, between the ribs, and we would then use an instrument to pull the ribs apart, enabling us to get into the cavity. There were times when a rib or two would crack. In certain cases, it was inevitable. Alternatively, we might remove a rib altogether and go into the chest from the bottom of that rib. Proceeding this way helped to prevent the unintentional cutting of any blood vessels. But it was more difficult to close the wound using this method, because of the missing rib.

This conservative approach to treating stab wounds of the chest suggested that, with a close watch of the patient, we might not have to operate whenever we saw a patient with stab wounds to the abdomen caused, for example, by the sharpened spoke of a bicycle.

Bicycle spokes had become the weapon of choice for many of the young local hoodlums. They would remove a spoke from a bicycle wheel, sharpen one end to a stiletto-thin point, put a cork on the other end to use as a handle, and then wield the spoke as a weapon. It was a favourite instrument of the street, readily available, cheap to make, and very dangerous. We occasionally saw patients who had suffered ten or fifteen stab wounds through the intestines.

At first, we would routinely open the patients, find each stab wound, and sew it up. Eventually, however, we decided to stop opening the abdomens. There were simply too many cases and too many stab wounds. Only when the large bowel had been pierced, or when there was excessive bleeding for other reasons, might there be problems if we did not operate. But the wounds in the small intestine caused by bicycle spokes generally sealed themselves. The bicycle-spoke stabbings were such a widespread phenomenon at that time that we saw some 2,000 cases during my eighteen months at Coronation. We published our observations and medical findings in a journal.

We also reported on some six hundred fractures of the jaw (mandible) that we treated with a particular type of external splint. Instead of wiring the teeth, we put pins on either side of the fracture and connected them to a cross-strip metal bar that held the fracture firmly in place.

In addition, we treated a number of cases of gunshot wounds and fractured skulls. Luckily, however, most of the weapons in the neighbourhood were not high-power calibre, and this meant that the wounds were relatively "clean." The bullets remained intact inside the body; they did not explode inside or cause damage too far away from the entry point. If pieces of broken skull had been pushed into the brain, we had to open the skull to remove the shattered pieces. There were also times when we were called upon to drain subdural hematomas. We either used burr holes or a trephine, a hollow circular drill.

We were white doctors in a black-patient-only hospital. The violence on the streets outside Coronation Hospital, unfortunately, became a source for our medical advances. We saw a great many trauma cases, especially on weekends. But, despite the violence in the neighbourhood, we never feared to drive to Coronation. We'd go out on emergency calls in the middle of the night through the black areas of town, responding to our medical oaths and our consciences rather than to the reports of violence that were becoming increasingly frequent about Johannesburg in 1950 South Africa.

"I want to thank you most sincerely for all you did for me over the past few weeks. It gave me great consolation and confidence knowing you were in the theatre. Sorry my appendix made you battle. I greatly appreciate all the trouble you took— from the consultation…to the booking of my room—and seeing that I got first class attention, which I assure you, I did."
—R. BENIGNUS, AUGUST 1968

CHAPTER 8 | # The "situation" in South Africa

W HEN I STUDIED MEDICINE in Johannesburg, not a single black student was enrolled in the university, let alone in the medical faculty. Blacks were prohibited from attending any university. South African Indians, too, were kept out of the universities until about 1940. As I mentioned earlier, if they wanted to study medicine, they had to do so in Ireland or India. If they studied in Ireland, their certificate would be readily recognized in South Africa. But those who went to India had to write a qualifying exam before they could get their licence.

Some years later, when I was established in Durban, I supported a campaign led by my friend, Ochie Gordon, to establish a medical school for non-whites in Durban. Of course, the government was not in favour of the idea, but their resistance could not prevail against Ochie's determined efforts. The school, based at King Edward VIII Hospital, was established in the early 1950s. Eventually the government funded the construction of a new medical school that included modern, well-equipped labs for physiology, chemistry, anatomy, and pathology. For the first few years, students who were accepted into first-year medicine had to undergo a two-year program of intense matriculation preparations. This enabled them to bridge their way into a medical program that was far more demanding than the high school studies the students were leaving. At the same time, the program provided incoming students with the prerequisites that they would need for the subjects they would soon be studying in medical school. I lectured at the King Edward VIII medical school and took part in seminar work with the students. It was both enjoyable and rewarding.

In the early years of the school, most of the students were Indians. Blacks were not as well prepared at first to handle the demands of the workload and, indeed, of the language. Aside from the fact that they only had access to an inferior education system, most of the black students were so poor that they did not have the appropriate facilities or environment at home in which to study. For example, a black student may have had to study by candlelight, on the floor, with many siblings at his elbow in a very small, crowded room. It was not very conducive to studying and learning. Eventually, though very slowly, blacks managed to overcome these disadvantages.

By the late 1980s, coloureds and the Indians were allowed to work as residents at Addington Hospital; blacks were still barred from doing so. That last colour bar at Addington was not dropped until the beginning of the last decade of the twentieth century. By the time Nelson Mandela was released from prison, in February 1990, black physicians were working at Addington as well.

❖ ❖ ❖

D. F. Malan's Afrikaner-dominated National Party won the national elections in 1948, driving the venerable and moderate Jan Smuts from power. With the passage of the Group Areas Act, Malan's party officially legislated apartheid, South Africa's national policy of racial separation. Over the next five years, a series of discriminatory and repressive laws were enacted, among which were the deeply symbolic and much hated pass laws that effectively confined the blacks to very narrowly defined geographical areas.

With the radical change in political conditions for blacks came an attendant change, for the worse, in social and economic conditions. The period at the end of World War II was the watershed: in truth, the political changes followed from, rather than caused, the economic changes. During the war, many blacks had left the outlying farmland to find work in either the mines or the cities, where jobs seemed to be plentiful. After the war, jobs became scarcer but the influx of men looking for work did not abate. Working in the mines was uncommonly difficult at the best of times, but it was particularly harsh for black men. They lived in hostels that were nothing more than shacks and shanties and were completely separated from their families. If the male worker was married, his wife and children lived back in his home city or town, generally not nearby. I have already mentioned that this was true for our servants as well— they lived away from their families and would not likely see them more than once or twice a year.

The system of apartheid was the social, legal, and political expression of Boer attitudes. But Great Britain was certainly not blameless in the unfolding structure of increasing legal repression. From the very beginning of its colonial rule and dominance in the Cape, starting in the early nineteenth century, Britain never insisted upon or attempted to create a bona fide system of education for the native African population. Without a system of good, meaningful, formal education, blacks were held down. Their horizons were kept deliberately narrow. The Afrikaners—with their entrenched feelings of superiority— insisted on keeping the blacks down and the British—who professed more liberal views—condoned the oppression and never did a thing to help the blacks. That system of oppression and exploitation, the product of malevolence on one side and indifference on the other, burdened the structure of South African society to its core with the increasing weight of discrimination, injustice, and inequity until, eventually, the structure crumbled in upon itself.

In 1961, South Africa declared itself a republic and officially broke away from the Commonwealth. Successive prime ministers of the National Party—Hendrik Verwoerd, B. J. Vorster, P. W. Botha—maintained and buttressed the apartheid policies. D. F. Malan even took the vote away from the coloureds when he created a tricameral parliament with separate legislative chambers for the whites, the coloureds, and the Indians. This discriminatory system doubly discriminated against blacks by not allowing them to have their own chamber—the entire black majority population of South Africa had no parliament, no political voice at all.

Blacks were relegated to Bantustans, small, segregated enclaves for blacks only. Blacks who lived in South Africa proper could only vote in Bantustans even if they had no personal, historic, or other connection there. Repression became total. This, of course, merely exacerbated the hatreds that were already taking hold. Violence on both sides became endemic as the only means of political discourse.

By 1968, when my son, Mike, left South Africa, violence was commonplace. A bomb exploded on the beach in Durban not too far from our home. We felt that violence was encroaching. From that time onward, blacks grew gradually more militant, both in terms of political organization and in terms of violent action. Trade unions for blacks were banned, along with the right to free association for political or employment purposes. The result was a tinderbox of emotion and frustration.

Many people agree that the turning point in the situation— a turning point that led to the eventual demise of the apartheid system—can be traced to the Sharpeville massacres in the spring of 1960, when police fired into a crowd and killed sixty-nine unarmed protesters. After the massacres, the government banned certain opposition groups; as a result, they all went underground. This decision, more or less, gave birth to the beginning of the armed, violent struggle by black and mixed-race groups against the government. In June 1964, Nelson Mandela, the leader of the banned African National Congress (ANC), was arrested on charges of trying to overthrow the government, tried, convicted and sentenced to life imprisonment.

From that point forward, South African society descended into a seemingly unstoppable spiral of disorder, crime, and violence. As an example, in 1976, ongoing protests in the black township of Soweto left 575 people dead over a period of eight months. In 1977, the charismatic political leader Steven Biko died while in police custody. Biko's death ignited a new conflagration of anger and violence. The cycle of repression and response became entrenched in a South African society that was full of danger and hate.

But "the winds of change" started to blow—albeit some two decades after Harold Macmillan said they would—with the election of premier of F. W. de Klerk in 1989. He began revoking the laws of oppression, lifted the ban on the opposition parties, and, most important of all, promised to release Nelson Mandela from his prison. By then, Mandela had been in jail for twenty-seven years. These and many other progressive measures by de Klerk eventually led to the election of Nelson Mandela, in 1994, as premier of South Africa.

By the time Mandela was elected, we had been living in Canada for six years and were observing developments from afar. When historians write about this period in South African history, they will truly marvel at the relative bloodlessness of the "coup." It was indeed a triumph of the human spirit and especially of the spirit of two men in particular: F. W. de Klerk and Nelson Mandela.

❖ ❖ ❖

As the National Party's series of repressive laws were being enacted in the 1950s, I became more and more convinced that I wanted to leave South Africa. I was very unhappy about the political situation. The South African Jewish community was generally anti-apartheid—when Nelson Mandela looked for an articling position as a lawyer, his first employer was Jewish—nonetheless felt powerless to change conditions for fear of repercussion. Some chose to leave; a few became anti-apartheid activists and some of them were imprisoned. In our circle of friends, we often talked about the political and social developments and many of us started planning to leave the country. Most of us were not political activists—our chief concern was for our families and for our children's futures. But there were exceptions. Helen Suzman stood out for her political activism and courage. I knew her husband, Mosie, a prominent internist in Johannesburg very well; to me, it seemed that they led quite separate lives.

In the late 1950s, South Africans across a wide spectrum began to look for ways to send money abroad in preparation for the day that they would no longer be living in South Africa. They had to be inventive about it because, apart from small fixed sums that were necessary for vacations, it was illegal to take or send money overseas. The government frowned on all attempts to remove funds from the country, punishing anyone caught and convicted of doing so with stiff jail terms and heavy fines. But people did so, nonetheless. The potential benefit seemed worth the risk. Some people paid a considerable commission to a third party for transporting funds abroad. Others bought as many dollars as they could on the black market and personally carried the funds out of the country. One much-talked-about case concerned a fellow who boldly—many at the time said recklessly—packed a suitcase with many thousands of dollars of hard American cash and decided, simply, to walk through the turnstile, as it were, and onto the airplane. Miraculously, he was not caught!

Some people bought gold Kruger coins and carried them out of the country. In those days, metal detectors had not yet been installed at the airports. As long as one was moderate in the amount of coins one carried, it could be done without arousing too much suspicion. Still others, who did business abroad, sent funds out of the country to pay for goods delivered or services rendered but on accounts that were artificially inflated.

Despite the government's best efforts to curb the removal of private funds from South Africa, individuals were not deterred from trying to do so. Indeed, the determination to accumulate funds outside of the country for a sunnier day inspired considerable ingenuity and creativity.

The injustice of the political and social situation was constantly on our minds, and our relationships with our servants was caring, respectful, and thoughtful. One example might illustrate the point. I received a call late one night from the police, advising us that our houseboy, John, had been arrested for brewing *chwala*, a homemade beer.

"We've got a chap—John—here. He says he works for you. Is that true?" came the gruff voice at the other end of the line.

"Yes, it is," I answered.

"We picked him up for selling his homemade brew. Are you willing to come get him?"

I immediately went down to the station to collect him. When I got there, I saw that John was in a state of obvious terror. He knew that the police could have beaten him, as was normally their routine in such situations. But they chose not to because of John's relationship to our family.

Around the same time, the Biko case was an extreme example of the treatment of blacks in the hands of the police. To my regret, some doctors were also implicated in Biko's beating death. The doctors examined him, saw the results of the beating, yet allowed the police to remove him from jail, even though it was clear Biko was in no condition to be moved. Some time later, these doctors were brought before the South African Medical Council for disciplinary hearings. They were reprimanded; one lost his licence for a year. But this was a very mild sentence in light of the fact that Biko lost his life.

From time to time, the district surgeon would call me to visit ill prisoners—mostly blacks—in the jail. The experience was unpleasant and, at times, harrowing. I would arrive at the jail. Approach the door. Ring to be let in. The door would open. I would step into a small antechamber. *Clang*. The door behind me would lock. A second door would open. I would step in and proceed in the company of a warder. *Clang*. The second door would shut. We would find the cell of the prisoner. Wait for the door to open. Step inside. The door would shut behind us. I would then examine the patient in his cell. After the examination, the procedure with the locked doors was repeated. I would then call the district surgeon to report my findings and diagnosis.

Despite the unpleasant setting, or perhaps more accurately on account of it, I never feared to report a true diagnosis.

By and large, the political divisions in society were also reflected in the medical establishment. Although it is somewhat of a generalization, I believe that the Afrikaner doctors were far more supportive of the regime and the apartheid system than the British doctors. An extreme example, the famous case of Dr. Wouter Basson, an Afrikaner cardiologist, comes to mind. He was called Dr. Death by people who served with him in the army. He was also compared to the notoriously cruel Nazi doctor Josef Mengele. Basson was the alleged founder and leader of Project Coast, a top-secret chemical and biological warfare program run by the army. It was said that his department researched, planned, and even executed the vilest forms of germ and other mass destruction experiments on political "undesirables."

Basson rejected the amnesty offered by the Truth and Reconciliation Commission headed by Archbishop Desmond Tutu, preferring instead to submit to a trial. Unbelievably, he was recently acquitted of the charges against him.

It should be observed that the Truth and Reconciliation Commission, established at the onset of black majority rule, was unique. Tell the truth and you were forgiven. It was, of course, a way of giving the whites an "out." The alternative would have brought chaos to the country because some of the very people who might otherwise have been charged for their involvement in the repressive apartheid crimes were still part of the state machinery that was bringing people to justice.

Even under the worst days of apartheid, the judicial system in South Africa, by and large, was worthy of respect. The Supreme Court was considered good and honourable. We happened to know a number of the legal luminaries of the upper courts: Alan Magid and David Friedman, both of the Supreme Court, and Solly Miller of the Court of Appeal. These men were exemplars of great integrity and never compromised conscience or principle for the sake of expedience. Nor did they buckle to the societal pressures that weighed on them from all sides.

We and our close personal friends were opposed to apartheid. But we felt we could not actively or politically do anything to change the system. That's the way it was for us. Rather than change the system, we chose to leave it.

"Three days ago I received your remarkable account 'no charge' and ever since I have been searching for the words, knowing their inadequacy, which would convey, somehow, the measure of my appreciation of this tremendous kindness. Not only have you revealed your skill as a surgeon and released me from pain, you have exposed your inner self, a high-minded, generous spirit, a rare combination. To be the fortunate recipient is a deeply moving experience for which I am very grateful."
—SHEVA HODES, JULY 1969

CHAPTER 9

Johannesburg General Hospital

AFTER EIGHTEEN MONTHS working at Coronation Hospital, I was transferred to the hospital for white patients only, Johannesburg General Hospital, the main teaching hospital in the city, affiliated with the University of Witwatersrand.

Not all of the staff were full-time. The professor of surgery worked full-time but did not always come into the wards. He spent more of his time in the labs and lecture halls teaching the registrars, interns, and undergraduates.

There were four surgical wards and each had a unit of four people: a chief, an assistant chief, a registrar, and a houseman. We alternated outpatient rounds with the chief and the assistant chief and did regular rounds at 8:00 every morning. It did not matter what we had done the previous night or in the early hours of the morning, we were all expected to make the morning rounds as a unit. A sister, the charge nurse, would come with us. We would do a round of the wards, seeing both the male and female patients.

The houseman would present the case, looking at his notes and developing his medical findings. The chief would then ask him questions concerning the most likely diagnoses, differential diagnoses, other possible investigations that might be warranted, and other possible treatments. The registrar would be on standby, for if the intern could not respond to the chief's queries, the chief would turn to him. I was never afraid to speak up, although some chiefs certainly tried to instill a sense of fear in all of us. There was simply no other way to learn. Moreover, I generally felt confident with the material.

With friends on the coast just outside Durban, South Africa, 1934. I'm first on the left, second row.

Playing tennis at the Durban Jewish Club, 1934.

With my fiancée, Lola Jankelson, and my parents, Judel and Malka Stein, 1945.

My in-laws, Moey and Freda Jankelson, in Oudsthoorn, South Africa.

With my bride, Lola, on our honeymoon, at Scottburgh, on the Natal Coast, South Africa. We were married 14 October 1945.

Swimming in the sea on our honeymoon at Scottburgh, South Africa.

Travelling through the highlands of Scotland in a Morris Minor we bought with £300 that Lola's father had sent us. He had won £1,000 in the Rhodesian sweepstakes and he shared it with his three daughters.

Lola, as a young girl, at about 19 years of age.

Lola dispensing during her apprenticeship at the Tryza Pharmacy, Pretoria, South Africa.

Lola, with our three children, Linda, David, and Mike, in our garden in Durban, around 1957.

Lola and me, with her two sisters, her parents, and all the children. Lola is sitting and I'm standing, far left. Lola's sister Adeline is sitting far right, and her other sister Annette is standing, third from the left, beside her husband, Max. My brother-in-law Syd is standing, far right.

The work was quite different at the General than it was at Coronation. Unlike we had at Coronation Hospital, we treated considerably fewer trauma victims at the General. By contrast, we dealt with surgical conditions more typically associated with a higher socio-economic patient base, such as duodenal ulcers, cardiac, respiratory, and orthopedic issues. But we saw some rather unusual cases as well.

One night an old man presented himself with an acute intestinal obstruction of the small bowel. With black patients, due to their living conditions, such an obstruction would likely be caused by a mass of round ascaris worms. But given this man's background and socio-economic standing, that diagnosis seemed far-fetched.

On opening the abdomen, we found a spherical mass in the small intestine, but could not move it. When we opened the intestine, however, out came an entire, peeled orange. The next morning, when I told the man what we had found he said, "So that's where it went!" Apparently he had peeled an orange and then bent down to fasten his shoelaces. When he stood up, the orange had disappeared. Apparently, our man had put the orange in his mouth to liberate his hands for tying his shoes. He had somehow forgotten about the orange, but even more remarkably, he did not realize he had swallowed it.

Another memorable experience involved a sick old lady, over eighty-years, old who had been admitted to the hospital at 2:00 a.m. with a perforated gastric ulcer. She urgently needed an operation; it was a true emergency. But when the anesthetist was asked to see the patient prior to surgery, he was troubled by her condition and called his chief to administer the anesthetic.

Jackie Douglas was my chief at the time. A colonel during the war, he was very well-known in the medical community and well-liked for both his demeanour and his medical mastery.

I called him to alert him to the situation. He told me to go ahead as it was not a difficult procedure, reminding me that I had done it several times before.

The professor of anesthetics arrived in the early hours. When he found himself opposite a "lowly" resident in the operating theatre, he was quite miffed that I, and not the chief surgeon, was standing beside him. He made certain to point out his displeasure to me and emphasized that he wished the surgery done as quickly as possible.

The woman was so thin, I went through the layers of skin and fat in one cut. I had not even needed an X-ray to help make the diagnosis. Today, all sorts of tests would be done prior to surgery, generally a waste of money and time, but dictated perhaps by the fear of litigation. I could actually hear and feel the air between her liver and the chest wall. After the incision, I immediately saw the hole in the stomach. So I took a piece of the omentum—a fatty sheet of tissue that normally acts as the "policeman" of the abdomen, creating a protective covering wherever a hole or infection occurs in the abdomen—put it on the hole, sewed four little stitches on the corners and left it in place. I then stitched through all the layers of skin, muscle and fat in one. I was finished in less than ten minutes.

They called me "Speedy Stein" after that.

I cannot say I was "summoned" to medicine or to surgery or even to vascular surgery in particular, but I can say, without any equivocation, that it was indeed a calling. It seemed I was born with the disposition that meshed well with the demands of surgical medicine. Thus, as a young doctor, I concentrated my efforts on developing and refining the skills that would enable me to become a top surgeon. I had good "surgical hands," good hand-eye coordination. I did not panic under pressure; I learned to be quite resourceful in tight situations and I could make quick decisions. One had always to be prepared for surprises in the operating room. You might open an abdomen, expecting to find an appendix problem, and suddenly finding yourself staring at something quite different.

For example, I remember a case, some years later, in which I was called on an emergency by a surgeon at Renishaw-Scottburgh Hospital down the south coast. He had opened the abdomen of a patient, thinking he was operating on an infected appendix, only to see instead a mass of black dead tissue. He was completely lost. So he called me at my home in Durban.

It's an hour-long drive to Renishaw, but I got there as quickly as I could. The patient had been anesthetized the entire time. I scrubbed, entered the theatre, and peered into the open abdomen. There was indeed an unusual mass of blackened dead tissue. It was the omentum, which had twisted on itself and become gangrenous. All I had to do was to lift it off the bowel and, with my finger and thumb, break through it at the top of the transverse colon, along a little protruding clump that was as wide as a finger. The entire pretzel-like tissue was dead; when I broke it off, there was no bleeding. It was a relatively simple procedure to remove the rather large, unpleasant-looking mass and throw it into the waste bucket. Because of my experience I had been able to identify the mystery mass. From that time forward, I have no doubt, that young Renishaw doctor would also be able to identify a dauntingly large, discoloured, twisted, mis-shapen clump of dead abdominal tissue wrapped around the intestines as the omentum.

After I returned from England in 1948, in addition to my work at Coronation and the General, I would also go once a week to Pietermaritzburg, which had no orthopedic surgeons, to assist with surgery there. I used to go with a colleague, Dr. "Moon" Mullins. Conditions in Pietermaritzburg were sometimes very primitive. In one case, I remember, a man had been in hospital for two years. He had been simply put into the recovery bed two years earlier and left there. Out of sight, out of mind. After two years, all his joints had contracted.

During this period, I once operated on a doctor attached to one of the "hit squads" in Angola. I knew that he had been one of the members of those squads. One came across many such people who had been in the army. Since there were no army surgeons in Durban, the army doctor would ask me to do the surgery for him. It was quite an interesting experience.

Toward the end of my three-year stint at the University of Witwatersrand Medical School, I applied to the South Africa Medical Council to be registered as a specialist surgeon. I had already completed eleven years of postgraduate training and experience in various hospitals in Europe and South Africa and felt that I was ready to open my own private practice. But the council refused my application on the basis that I had not yet done the required two years of family practice. They ordered me to do six more months of general practice, irrespective of all my other experience.

In spite of all the hard work and long hours, though, I still found time to play bridge and keep up with my friends, enjoying a social life both in Durban and in Johannesburg.

*"After my examination yesterday by Dr. Berkowitz,
I must write this brief personal message to you that
you may know that I shall be always mindful of the miracle
brought about through your wonderful operation.
"This perfect healing and complete recovery...has given me
a new life. Words cannot express my gratitude."*
—DOROTHY DUNCAN ANDREW, MAY 1970

CHAPTER 10 **To Lusaka and back**

SINCE THE SOUTH AFRICAN Medical Council had insisted that I do an additional six months training in family practice medicine before getting my specialist license, I had no choice but to look around for a posting. I found it in Lusaka, Northern Rhodesia, (now Zambia). A good friend of mine, Lazar Molk, who had interned with me at Addington Hospital in Durban, was in practice in Lusaka. He asked me to come and work with him there. He wanted to take some vacation time and needed someone who could step into his practice with relative ease. I was grateful for the offer and accepted. It seemed as though it would be an interesting experience for my family and me.

As Northern Rhodesia was still a British colony, my UK and South African credentials were readily accepted by the governing college and I was able to take over for Molk. It was 1952. Lola and I packed up once again, put Linda and our son, Mike—who was born in Johannesburg on March 11, 1951—into the car, and headed to Lusaka. By this time, Linda was four years old and Mike was one. We travelled by ourselves, a young family of four, right into the *bundu*, the unpopulated, uncultivated, wild countryside. In retrospect, it was quite remarkable. Lola, as usual, deserved a great deal of credit. Our route was from Johannesburg to Lusaka, through Salisbury and Bulawayo.

The journey turned out to be quite an experience. It was a long trip, not without risk, in very hot, humid, tropical summer conditions. The roads were mostly dirt, unpaved and unfinished. There were some exceptions, however. The better roads had asphalt strips for the tires. To our more modern eyes, these roads were an odd sight. The strips of tarmac formed two parallel black lines that, after a rainfall, were raised considerably higher than the rest of the road. The rain, which often fell in torrents, simply washed the dirt away. The tarmac strips thus became like smooth, raised platforms on a bumpy and often muddy road. If one's tires came off the strips, it was very difficult to get back on them again. It gave new meaning to the term "travelling on the highway."

Two roadside episodes on that trip stand out in my mind.

The first occurred as we were motoring along near the midpoint of our journey, when the car suddenly ground to a halt and the engine died. Try as hard as I might, I could not get the engine to ignite. I knew very little about the anatomy of any system other than that of a human and felt quite helpless to diagnose, let alone repair, the problem with our car. So, Lola and I sat rather nervously with our two small children in our disabled vehicle on the shoulder of the road, in the sweltering heat, waiting for someone to come along, take pity on us, stop his car, and offer help.

Eventually, such a person did come along. Fortunately, he knew something about cars. He lifted the bonnet (hood) and found that one of the battery terminal connections had cracked. His solution was quite novel and effective. He took a Rhodesian penny from his pocket. The penny was like a mini copper doughnut, with a hole in the middle. Our rescuer placed the penny over one of the terminals, across the crack, and fixed it in place with a nut and bolt. This worked so well that the penny remained on the damaged battery terminal until we returned to South Africa many months later.

The second episode also involved the car, but was far more dangerous and hair-raising. Thank God the car was fully operational by then.

We were coming round a wide bend in the road, at a not insignificant speed, when suddenly we came face to face with an enormous bull elephant standing in the middle of the road. I jammed on the brakes and was able to bring the car to a noisy but total stop very close to the gigantic elephant, too close for comfort. Ours and, undoubtedly, his, too. I nearly hit him.

The elephant stared at me. I stared back at him. We stared at each other. He started stamping his feet. Lola held her breath and the children, miraculously, retained their composure and stayed very quiet. Or perhaps, like me, they were just too frightened to say anything. Many were the stories we had heard of rampaging bull elephants. There was no predicting his mood or his movements. But we did know for certain that we had better steer clear of him immediately. I put the car into reverse and very slowly, so as not to startle the monstrous pachyderm blocking our path, I got far enough away that I could no longer smell his breath. Thankfully, as the distance between us increased, the elephant left the road and headed off into the bush. My heart had been pounding so hard, my chest hurt. When my heart rate and breathing returned to normal, we resumed our journey onward to Lusaka.

After two days in the car and one night in a hotel in Bulawayo, we arrived in Lusaka and went straight to Molk's house. He had rented an apartment for us and before long we were installed there. A maid helped us with the flat and the children. But Lola ran the house and did the cooking and the housework essentially by herself.

One of the differences between Rhodesia and South Africa that we discovered soon after our arrival was that Rhodesian insects were significantly larger than their South African counterparts. All of them, it seemed were much bigger: spiders, cockroaches, even the flies.

The Lusakan lifestyle was typically colonial, centred around the club and the bar. On Saturday nights we would go to the club to dance and have a drink. Lusaka was a friendly and open small city with one main downtown street.

During our short stay in Lusaka we got to know all the "important people." The mayor at that time, Sam Fisher, was Jewish. When he died, his nephew, Jack Fisher, replaced him as mayor. Jack eventually moved to San Diego and we are friendly to this day. We also met Roy Welensky, who was the Prime Minister of Northern Rhodesia. He was a very large man, whose first line of work was as a train driver. He changed careers, becoming the heavyweight boxing champion of Rhodesia, and then parlayed his boxing into politics, becoming prime minister. When Northern Rhodesia, Southern Rhodesia, and Nyasaland amalgamated, he became the new country's first governor general and was subsequently knighted. But the newly amalgamated entity did not last very long and soon split into three separate countries: Northern Rhodesia became Zambia; Southern Rhodesia became Zimbabwe, and Nyasaland became Malawi. Ian Smith became prime minister of Southern Rhodesia and effected a unilateral declaration of independence in 1965 until he was forced by the UK to surrender power.

We led a very unpressured, interesting life during those six months in Lusaka. Molk's practice was a conventional family practice for whites. But because Northern Rhodesia was a tropical country, I had to deal with certain occasions and certain medical conditions that were somewhat different than those I had known in South Africa.

One day, for example, a woman brought her child to the office to see me. The child had a very angry-looking rash— little red pimples, tiny little boils, all of which were covered with pustule ends—on a particular spot on the body. I diagnosed the child's condition as impetigo and prescribed treatment for it accordingly. The mother disagreed with my diagnosis, but took the medication and left.

A week later, the woman came to me with a bottle containing tiny, white, worm-like things and said, "That's the impetigo."

I had never seen anything like it before, nor had I even heard of it. Those "worms" were the larvae of the putzi fly. They had laid their eggs on wet clothing that had been drying out in the sun. When the clothing came in contact with the child's skin, the larvae burrowed into the skin and produced what looked like a typical impetigo. Inside each little red boil was the larva of a hatching fly. When you squeezed the boil, out came the larva. That was my introduction to putzi flies.

It took a while to become familiar with the medical conditions that were unique to this part of Africa. For example, whenever someone presented with a fever, one had to assume it was malaria-related and not flu-related. Malaria was so widespread that our first test was always to determine whether a fever was part of a presenting malaria. The test was a simple microscope examination of a drop of the patient's blood. We did it right in the office. And we all soon learned to take anti-malarial pills on a regular basis.

While I was in Lusaka, I also performed all the surgery at Molk's practice. There were no practising specialists in Lusaka, so any major problem was sent to South Africa or, occasionally, to Salisbury in Southern Rhodesia for treatment.

Ironically, no sooner had we arrived in Lusaka than I received a letter from the South African Medical Council telling me that they had approved my application for specialty certification after all. In view of my long hospital training, they had decided to waive the additional six months of family practice. But, since we had already made the journey north, we decided to remain for the full six months that I had promised Molk. At the end of my term, he asked me to stay on with him and practise medicine in Lusaka, but we decided to go back to Durban. Molk eventually left Lusaka and settled in Denver where he re-qualified and established a successful practice as a specialist in internal medicine. His son is a cardiologist and also lives in Denver.

At the end of March 1953, we headed back to South Africa in the same car we had arrived in, using the same broken battery that had brought us to Lusaka a half-year earlier. On the way home, we stopped at the magnificent Victoria Falls, the tallest and broadest waterfalls in the world, holding our children tightly in our arms as we stood literally in the spray of that miraculous natural wonder. We stayed overnight at the Victoria Falls Hotel. While Lola and I were at dinner and the two little children supposedly safe in their beds, we were startled and somewhat amused to see them stroll into the dining room, in their pyjamas, looking for us.

Our lives were an adventure, or so it seemed to us as we got back into the car to continue our journey southward and home. In South Africa, we stopped at Lola's parents home in Johannesburg so that our children could visit their grandparents.

Once back in Durban, we again moved in with my parents until we managed to get an apartment on Musgrave Road. I had already arranged, in advance, to start work at Addington Hospital as the first part-time registrar in the surgery department. I set up my office at the Colonial Mutual Buildings on West Street, the main business street in downtown Durban. I could not have done so without the assistance of my aunt Gertie Hackner, Uncle Oscar's widow. She lent me £25 each month to pay the initial rent. Uncle Oscar had died previously of a ruptured appendix.

I was now finally ready to put out my surgeon's shingle in Durban, where my parents had settled from Lithuania more than twenty-six years earlier. I was on the register as a specialist in surgery and practising in Durban, married, with two children, and determined to become as good a surgeon as my skills and temperament would permit.

Mannie Stein, M.B.B.Ch (Wits. Univ.) F.R.C.S. (Edin.), D.G.O. (Trinity Univ. Dublin), D.A. (RCP & S. I).

I was not yet thirty-three.

*"You are talking about a special person when
you talk about Mannie Stein...
"We were on a Habonim camp in Amanzimtoti,
a coastal village not far from Durban and he was very quick
to show us his newly-acquired knowledge as a first year medical
student. When a foreign body went into a young boy's eye,
Mannie had to demonstrate to all of us little boys what a great
doctor he was, albeit only in first year medicine, by turning his
eye inside out. Needless to say, we were not only shocked but
most impressed with his medical prowess and from that day on,
he became our hero.
"I think his greatest and most loved trait was the human touch,
whether you were his patient or not. If you were his friend
he made it his business to get involved in your problems and,
if necessary, interfere with whomever was treating you.
"I was scared and reluctant to proceed with bypass surgery that
was necessary twenty-two years ago. One Saturday afternoon
Mannie arrived at my home with the physician and general
practitioner and laid down the law to me that I had to have this
operation. After I left the hospital, I had various problems with
chest and leg leakage. Mannie would come to my home daily to
dress the wounds and to deal with the problems.
I did not ask for this. He automatically assumed that,
as my friend, this is what he should be doing for me.
Even though Mannie has been gone from Durban for some
time, he is remembered and loved by, at least,
the whole Jewish population there..."*
—MORRIS SCHAFFER, JULY 2001

CHAPTER 11

Medical practice in Durban

I N MY PRIVATE PRACTICE at the Colonial Mutual
Buildings on West Street, I shared office space
with Barry Adams, whose specialty was internal medicine and
whom I had known since childhood. We went through high
school and medical school together. He was also on the same
ship as Lola and I when I went to study in the UK.

Our office was quite small. We had an examination room
each, a common reception room, and a consulting area. Barry
and I were fortunate to acquire an outstanding secretary who
took pity on us and worked, at the outset, for a modest salary.
She stayed with us for several years.

Not surprisingly, some of the established physicians and surgeons in Durban resented our arrival. I was told more than once
that we would fall on our faces, that there were already enough
surgeons in Durban and that we would not make the grade. To
prove the established surgeons and other naysayers wrong was
enough incentive for me—I was determined to be an excellent
surgeon. And after a relatively short period of time my practice
became quite busy. Naturally, because I was getting referrals that
were no longer going to them, some of the older, more senior
surgeons resented my success. Durban's doctors were now also
sending their patients to me, too.

But it was indeed gratifying to prove relatively quickly that
I could indeed make the grade. By the end of our first year, I
no longer needed to borrow the rent money from my aunt. In
fact, I was able to repay her the whole £300 that I had bor-
rowed interest-free.

I tried to get an appointment in a hospital, but it was

difficult. As I have already said, the two main hospitals in Durban were the King Edward VIII, the hospital for Indians and blacks, and Addington, the hospital for whites and coloureds. Addington had three surgical wards then and, as usual, each ward was staffed by a chief, an assistant, and a houseman. The three chiefs at that time were Messers. Radford, Warner, and King. The King Edward VIII Hospital had similar levels of staffing.

The typical route for appointment at Addington began with an appointment as an assistant surgeon at King Edward. After a time, when there was a vacancy at Addington, one rotated there. King Edward was seen very much, at that time, as a stepping stone to a position at Addington, which offered greater potential for financial security.

At the beginning I had very little surgical work to do. So I went to Addington whenever I could to help out in the three surgical units. In this way I kept my hands in the métier, as it were, literally and metaphorically. Some of the surgeons appreciated that I was willing to do the night work for them.

I also made it a high personal priority to watch or assist Mr. Aubrey Radford as often as I could. He was the most outstanding surgeon I have ever seen operate, including the many surgeons I subsequently saw operate all over the world. He was the first surgeon trained in Birmingham to come to South Africa.

Occasionally, Mr. Radford would consult with me on certain of his cases. One time he asked me to see an older woman in the hospital on whom he had performed gall bladder surgery. The wound had given way and the bowel had popped out into the bed. He phoned me about 2:00 in the morning and asked that I go and stitch it up for him. Naturally, I did, and the patient recovered. In her mind, she believed that I had saved her life. But I did only what any other surgeon in that situation would have done. The sense of vulnerability and the accompanying feeling of relief at recovery often translated into exaggerated but heartfelt and sincere expressions of appreciation from patients. Subsequently, she asked her friend, one of Durban's rabbis, to thank me. It was all a bit embarrassing.

In addition to being the senior surgeon at Addington Hospital, Radford was also the surgeon to the South African Railways and Harbours and to King George V Hospital, which, with some 2,000 beds, was the largest tuberculosis hospital in the southern hemisphere.

Two years after we opened our office, in 1954, I obtained the post of assistant surgeon at King Edward VIII Hospital. My chief then was a chap named Ike Goldberg. We saw far more trauma cases at King Edward than at Addington. But a short while later, not more than six months, I transferred to Addington as an assistant surgeon. In time I became the senior surgeon at Addington Hospital. That appointment caused Goldberg to become very upset with me. He had hoped that I would take over his practice, but I could not overlook the opportunity to work at Addington. It amounted to a promotion.

My responsibilities in the hospital were part-time, and I was paid an honorarium for my work there. Junior surgeons received £250 per year; the seniors received £500. But I spent a great deal more time at the hospital than was commensurate with the appointment and was given a fair amount of surgery at Addington to do on my own. After a while, I was given the more complicated cases, performing much of the surgery on our own wards and helping out with the orthopedic surgery as well because there was only one orthopedic surgeon at the time. Eventually Radford retired and was replaced as chief of the surgery ward by Lawrence Pearson. I became Pearson's assistant.

In my early years of practice, there were no surgeons in the country areas around Durban. So I would fly from Margate on the south coast to Empangeni on the north coast, and to Estcort inland to deal with emergencies. I chartered a little plane, usually a Piper cub. I remember once flying to Estcort with my son, Mike. It was winter and there was snow on the ground. Mike, who was around six years old, had never seen snow before. When he got off the plane, he immediately dove into the snow and rolled around in it happily and giddily, like a little puppy. As the years went by, these country areas were serviced by their own surgeons and my flying days came to an end. It was around this same time, in 1955, that our younger son, David, was born.

In 1958, after five years in practice, I became too busy to cope adequately, so I looked around for a partner. I found Roy Wise, a first-class surgeon who had been trained at the Postgraduate Medical School in Hammersmith, London, England. We remain close friends to this day. My cousin Gerald Hackner, who was also my accountant, drew up the partnership agreement. But before he asked me to sign the document he said to me, "You don't really need one." In the twenty-seven years that we were partners, I do not think I ever looked at that agreement.

Roy soon built up his own practice and was very seldom able to help me out except when we needed two surgeons for any procedure, such as excising a rectum or a difficult vascular surgery.

Therefore we decided that we needed a third partner and started looking around for one at the medical schools. We were determined to maintain our high standards and we felt that by conducting our search at the medical faculty, we would be able to do so.

Eventually, we came to an agreement with Harold Duncan who was acting professor of surgery at Pretoria University. He too was an instant success and he added his academic stature to our practice as well as his skill. He developed a large Afrikaner practice even though he was English. Coming from Pretoria, however, he was fluent in Afrikaans as well.

By the time I retired nearly thirty years later, in 1985, we had taken on a fourth partner, Graham Dawber. He too was an excellent surgeon, though he had a gruffer bedside manner with his patients. He did all our colonoscopy and gastroscopy work.

When Aubrey Radford retired from his post as chief surgeon for the South African Railways and Harbours, Roy Wise and I were appointed in his place. In turn, I elected Wise to be the senior Railways surgeon so that I would not have to do the bulk of the surgery there by myself. By this time, Duncan had become part-time surgeon to the South African Defence Forces in Durban. This was an interesting appointment that brought us all into contact with the army.

In 1960, I was appointed honorary surgeon to J. G. Croakes Hospital in Renishaw on the south coast of Natal at Scottburgh, about forty miles from Durban. It was here that I was called in the night to "rescue" what was believed by a surprised surgeon to be a routine appendicitis but turned out to be the dead blackened mass of the abdominal omentum. One of the incidental benefits of this appointment was that some of the general practitioners in the area would now reserve some of their cases for me rather than sending them to Durban.

By this time I had also been appointed Visiting Consultant Surgeon to King George V Hospital and this is where I learned a great deal of chest surgery from Radford. Interestingly, I never worried about contracting tuberculosis. I worked in the hospital for many years and I was there at least once a week. All the wards were full of TB patients, but we never immunized ourselves against the disease. We simply never thought about it. Living in a country where the disease was endemic, there were always a few ambient TB germs floating in the air. We must have inhaled them. Over the years, therefore, we had probably developed some sort of inherent immunity.

*"I would like to take this opportunity of thanking you
for all you have done for me during the past few weeks.
Your skill as a surgeon—your kindness and care of me
as a patient and your very high standards of medicine and
personal qualities have all been a great incentive to get well,
remain cheerful and resume all normal activities
with added zest."*
—RUDY SHAVE, NOVEMBER 1972

Chapter 12

On the cutting edge

T HE GREAT PROFESSOR Jannie Louw performed his first graft on an aortic aneurysm in Cape Town in 1956. I began similar work in Durban in 1957 when I performed my first femoral graft on a newspaper columnist, who subsequently wrote about the procedure in the local newspaper. Vascular surgery began to appear in Johannesburg and Pretoria around that time as well. There were only few of us doing vascular surgery in South Africa at the time.

In 1959, I decided to go London to see how the best in the world were doing vascular surgery. Thankfully, by then, we were able to travel by plane. I thus left my seafaring days officially behind me. I wanted to go to the UK to study with Charles Rob, a leading surgeon in the vascular field. I hadn't been back there since 1948, when vascular surgery was just coming into being. It interested me and I wanted to pursue it. St. Mary's Hospital in London was one of the best places to learn more about the advances in this area of surgery. Rob's assistant was a surgeon named Felix Eastcott and both doctors had established international reputations in this new and burgeoning field.

On the way to England, we stopped in Israel. We visited with my brother Havis who was working for the Israel Water Planning Company as District Engineer for Drainage in Upper Galilee. When we arrived there, he took some time away from his engineering duties to be our guide for an eight-day full-length tour of the country. He packed us into a Jeep and we drove from the Galilee in the north to the Sinai desert in the south, traversing as much of the young country as possible.

In London, for six weeks I concentrated purely on learning more and more about vascular work that dealt with the peripheral arteries. Afterward, on my return to Durban, I felt much more qualified to undertake these procedures. It was then that I performed my first replacement of an aneurysm of the abdominal aorta.

In those days, vascular work was very difficult, owing in part to the relative infancy of the field, which really only began to come into its own around 1953 or 1954. There were many problems caused by the suture materials. We did not, for example, have eyeless needles. Because we had to thread the needles, the hole made with the needle was smaller than the double-threaded gut we were using. Today, of course, one uses eyeless needles. The thread is clipped onto the needle and the resulting hole is the same thickness as the thread. In the early 1950s we also used the very small sutures that were used for eye surgery. Working with these tiny needles and hard Teflon graft in a deep cavity splashed with a lot of blood in dealing with a ruptured aneurysm was very difficult and time-consuming.

We did not have Dacron in those early days to sew as grafts onto the vein or artery we were repairing. At first, Rob used nylon tubes that his wife had made for him out of ordinary nylon sheeting. Unfortunately, the nylon was very porous. The blood would soak through and it would bleed like the devil. To control the bleeding and maintain the patient required a great deal of blood and patience.

After nylon, we used Teflon as the grafting material. But Teflon was not an ideal substance because it was very hard. Its one great virtue was that it was not porous and this meant one did not have the problem of excessive bleeding. But it was so hard and brittle that, at times, it ulcerated and broke into the surrounding areas, causing other tremendous problems. The most serious problem was that of the bowel adhering to the suture line in the graft and ulcerating. This, in turn, would cause severe bleeding that frequently led to the death of the patient. As a substitute, therefore, we tried to use homografts, that is, grafts from a cadaver or from organ donors. This was an extremely trying procedure because it necessarily entailed obtaining consent both from relatives of the deceased, and also from the authorities, who were often not very cooperative. We spoke to the faculty at the medical school that by now existed in Durban to see if we could obtain, for example, an aorta soon after death under sterile conditions, freeze-dry it, and store it for future use.

One case of a ruptured aneurysm of the abdominal aorta stands out in my memory. I received a phone call at home one evening from a physician whom I knew. He told me, briskly but firmly, that his patient, Reverend Hugh Yule, an older man, had suffered a ruptured aneurysm. He was calling from the reverend's home. "I've called an ambulance," he said. "They're taking him to the hospital. "The doctor's last words to me were "He's dying, Mannie."

I arranged for the ambulance to bring the reverend straight up to the operating room. His situation was so grave, there was simply no time for the usual intake procedures. I had also alerted the hospital staff and an anesthetist. All was ready when the reverend arrived at the hospital. The attendants put him fully clothed onto the operating table. I cut off his clothes and the staff prepped him as quickly as they could.

We couldn't find a pulse; his blood pressure was nil. I opened his abdomen. We used no anesthetic—there just wasn't time. The abdomen was completely bloodless; in effect, he was already gone. I felt his aorta and, by a stroke of good luck, was able to detect a faint pulse. I put one clamp above the aneurysm and another below it on the two sides going to the legs. I then inserted a needle into his vena cava and pumped in four pints of O negative blood. I had no time to even ensure the blood was compatible. In dire emergencies, one can use non-compatted blood because there is so little blood in the patient that adverse reactions seldom occur.

An instant later, the anesthetist said, "I can get a pulse." It was at that point that he started his work and put the reverend to sleep. And I replaced the blown-out area of the aorta with a graft. The freshly infused blood had the desired effect of bringing up his blood pressure to a promising 100 milligrams systolic. By then, the anesthetist was able to find a vein. The replacement graft was completed very rapidly and Reverend Yule made a full recovery.

A year later a stained glass window was installed in his church in my honour. Lola and I attended the ceremony and were deeply moved by the attention given to us and by the emotion of the moment.

In 1960, I returned to the UK to study with Robert Milnes-Walker, whose specialty was doing porto-caval shunts, in Bristol. These shunts are needed in situations where a patient has varicose veins at the lower end of the gullet arising from a diseased liver. If the veins rupture, the patient 's bleeding cannot be easily stopped without lowering the pressure in the liver. The way to do that is to join the vena cava to the portal vein, the vein that goes through and drains the liver. The pressure in the vein to the liver is high; in the vena cava, it is low. Thus the vena cava and the portal vein have to be joined. It is not an easy procedure.

I had seen someone try to do this procedure in Johannesburg in the early 1950s. The extensive bleeding required many pints of blood and the mortality rate was very high. Milnes-Walker had developed a technique to deal with the situation and he was very skilled at it. I phoned him from London and asked him if I might observe the next porto-caval procedure. He readily agreed and invited me to join him at the surgery scheduled for two days hence and arranged for the registrar to meet me at the train station. When I arrived at the hospital, Milnes-Walker was waiting for me with the rather sheepish announcement that he had already begun the surgery, but had stopped where he was, still at the early stages of the procedure, so as not to finish before I was able to join him.

I immediately gowned, scrubbed, joined him in the theatre and observed as he worked. He completed the surgery in an hour and a half. In other hospitals around the world, the procedure would have taken up to five hours. And he used one or two pints of blood instead of the five or more that were being used in the conventional surgeries.

When I returned to Durban, I demonstrated the Milnes-Walker porto-caval shunt method for my colleagues at King Edward VIII Hospital, where there were many such cases of liver disease due to alcohol-related cirrhosis.

Over time, of course, this method was further simplified. Milnes-Walker used to open the right side of the chest, split the diaphragm down the middle, and expose the whole of the liver to get a good view of everything. Subsequently, we found we could do the procedure with a little cut. That way, we did not have to dislocate the organs. Procedures evolved and things improved for the patients and for the surgeons.

In 1961, I went to Boston to observe the vascular work of a chap called Robert Linton and to the medical school at Columbia to observe another vascular expert named Moore. From there I went to Houston to observe Denton Cooley and Michael Debakey. Debakey was considered the world's best vascular surgeon, although to my eye, it appeared that Cooley was better technically. Debakey wrote a tremendous amount on the subject and would send me his literature, his annual reports on the surgery that took place in his hospital. Debakey once went to the Soviet Union to operate on Boris Yeltsin.

Linton, Moore, Cooley, and Debakey were pioneers in vascular work. I wanted to learn from them and bring back to my patients and my medical community the benefits of their medical courage and pioneering spirit. To this end, I would travel once a year seeking further knowledge of the latest in surgical advancements in order to constantly refine, upgrade, and improve my surgery. My partners did not mind. The vascular work I observed in Houston, for example, was extremely instructive. I stayed there for three weeks to study the work of Debakey and Cooley, who together were handling a large number of cases. Similarly, I stayed for a while at the UCLA hospital to observe the vascular work being done there. I left the practice for six to eight weeks at a time, but always returned with better medicine, as it were.

On one trip to London I went to study the kidney transplant method perfected by Ralph Shakman at the postgraduate school in London and brought that methodology back to Durban. Roy Wise and I subsequently performed the kidney transplants in Durban at Addington Hospital. These procedures were already being done in Johannesburg by Bertie Myburgh, who had excellent results by world standards.

On another trip to London, I visited with Ronald Raven, a senior surgeon at the London Cancer Hospital. He had his practice in a house on Harley Street. On the ground floor were his consulting rooms, on the second floor was his dining room, and on the top floor, he had his living quarters. He was a bachelor and his sister, who happened also to be the Senior Nursing

Sister of Great Britain, lived with him. Every time I went to London I would have dinner with him. His butler would greet us at the door. It was all so formal and so aristocratically British! We had sherry in the sitting room before dinner. On the occasions that he came to Durban, he always stayed with us.

Michael Debakey also stayed with us in Durban when he came through on a lecture tour.

Christian Barnard, easily one of South Africa's most popularly known vascular surgeons, was a bit junior to me in years and experience. While he was well-liked in the media, he wasn't very well-liked in the medical fraternity because he took advantage of his position. Moreover, many of us were critical of him because he never properly acknowledged Professor Jannie Louw who taught him, who pushed him ahead, who sent him to the US to learn cardiac surgery, and then brought him back to South Africa. Barnard's fame went to his head.

When the inaugural meeting of the Peripheral Vascular Society was convened, we elected Bertie Myburgh as president. Barnard was unhappy with us, but we did not much care. We voted according to merit, not popularity. Myburgh subsequently became vice-chancellor of the University of Witwatersrand in Johannesburg.

In the mid-1960s, many babies in Europe were born with only partial limbs or without any limbs at all as a result of their mothers having taken the drug thalidomide, used by expectant mothers to combat nausea during pregnancy. Professor Sulama in Helsinki became well-known for his reconstructive work on these babies. I decided to meet with him to see some of his work. He too was very kind to us and entertained Lola and me lavishly.

On another occasion I travelled to Stockholm. At that time, balloon catheters designed in Stockholm by Dr. Sven-Ivar

Seldinger, were being used for removing clots in blood vessels and grafts. I wanted to observe his procedures and to talk to him about the use of the catheter. He was very helpful and very friendly.

Before we could get the Seldinger catheter in Durban, we had to improvise. I did so with the best material we had. Thus, I began making balloon catheters for the hospital by tying a small piece of a condom onto a uretic catheter. And it worked reasonably well. By now I was the senior surgeon at Addington, consulting surgeon to King George V Hospital, consulting surgeon to Renishaw, and surgeon for the South African Railways and Harbours. At one stage, I was also the consulting surgeon to King Edward VIII Hospital, but I withdrew from that appointment. I kept the other four appointments until I retired in 1985.

My schedule was full. Twice a week I'd operate at Addington for two sessions. Twice a week I'd operate in my private practice. I'd go to King George Hospital once a week and to Renishaw Hospital once every fortnight. On occasion I'd operate at St. Aidan's, the Indian hospital, and then I had my consulting to do. I had to see my many patients. The days were full. We would start operating, on the dot, at 7:30 in the morning. I left my home around 6:00 a.m. and returned often past 9:00 p.m. I began to realize I could do without sleep. I could probably go two nights without sleeping and still work three days.

Despite my busy and hectic schedule, I had no regrets. I aspired to be at the top of the field and so I devoted the time that was required. But it came at a price. I hardly ever saw my children. I left before they were awake; I came home when they were in bed. This went on for a long time. That was the life I had carved out as a surgeon. But I could not have done so without Lola's full understanding. She carried the main weight of raising our children. The children's character, generosity, integrity, and profound goodness are a lasting testament and memorial to Lola's patience, love, diligence, and strength.

By 1965 I could report on more than five hundred aortic aneurysms that I had repaired. There were very few South Africans doing vascular surgery then. In the earlier days, we attempted all sorts of procedures to cope with aneurysms. We tried to remove them; we tried to pack them with various materials, we even tried to get homografts from cadavers. Today, the procedure is relatively easy using a piece of Dacron plastic.

We were in the vanguard of the field in South Africa, taking risks when it was necessary, innovating when there was no alternative, constantly pushing the frontiers of surgical work in South Africa forward. We did the best we could with the materials and the knowledge we had. I never experienced self-doubt, or fear, or loss of nerve during any of the procedures I performed. If I had, I would have "lost it." I would have lost the purposeful, almost stubborn, resolve, so vital to all surgeons, to work, indeed persevere, under conditions of extreme risk and pressure.

I reached the peak of my skills as a surgeon when I was somewhere between my late thirties and late fifties. During that time the surgery was as varied and as complicated as it was frequent. For example, we performed many surgeries on the carotid arteries. The difficulty in this surgery was to maintain continuous circulation to the brain while the blood flow in the artery was clamped off. The blood flow cannot be stopped for more than three minutes or the brain dies.

To deal with this problem, we used an assistive technique known as hypothermia, namely, dropping the patient's temperature significantly to slow down the patient's circulation. This hypothermic procedure would gain us an extra four or five minutes to work on the carotid artery. In the beginning, and relative to today, our hypothermic methods were quite crude. We anesthetized the patient with a tube down the throat, put him or her in a bath, and filled the bathtub with ice. We then put a thermometer into the patient's rectum to ensure that we would get a more accurate rectal temperature. When the temperature fell to the mid-20 degrees Celsius, we removed the patient from the bath, put him or her on the table, kept the body cool, and then opened the neck to work on the artery.

Nowadays, one doesn't worry about hypothermic procedures. One merely bypasses the carotid. But at that time, those extra four or five minutes were crucial. It meant the difference between the patient living or dying. And yet, as I write the words, they carry a far greater drama than when I was actually in the theatre operating on a patient with my eyes on both the patient's prone body and the clock. I simply did not allow myself to become emotional. It could have led to a disaster for the patient.

Another emerging procedure that I explored was the use of pressure chambers in the treatment of gangrene as well as during certain other operations. To learn from the top practitioners in the field, I visited Professor Charles Illingworth in Glasgow and Professor I. Boerema in Amsterdam. Their work was at the forefront in the use of pressure chambers and it was important to consult with them in order to reproduce their methods successfully back in Durban.

The fact that I was able to innovate, to pioneer, to be bold rather than reticent, gives me a great deal of satisfaction today. I was in a position to try new procedures because I was a senior surgeon whose credentials were in place and recognized by my peers. I wasn't afraid of a lawsuit, although, to be sure, I did not encourage one either. But I was confident in my skills and in my judgment. And I was always cognizant of the opportunities, when they presented, to push the frontiers of medicine.

The work of Peter Martin, a surgeon in the postgraduate school of medicine at Hammersmith in London, illustrates the point. He started interventionist procedures on cases of badly ruptured aortic aneurisms. His first nine cases died. If he had not been an accomplished, experienced, senior surgeon he could not have continued. In the first place, he would have probably given up. Secondly, he would have probably been sued. But his tenth case survived. Martin had persisted and persevered. Someone had to do it. He had the disposition and the skill to do so.

Professor James Learmonth performed his first patent ductus—the procedure to treat "blue baby" syndrome, in which the patent vessel between the lung and the heart must be tied off—in Edinburgh. The patient died on the table because Learmonth couldn't control the bleeding. Eyeless needles had not yet been invented for surgical use. If someone else had tried the procedure, and the patient died, there would have been an outcry. But because it was Learmonth, a person of unquestionable stature, people understood why he persisted in attempting what was clearly a risky procedure. He was trying to push the state of the art forward.

Similarly, Aubrey Radford pioneered much of the chest surgery in Durban during his work on tubercular cases at King George V. As one of the senior surgeons in Durban, I felt I could withstand criticism for bad results in new, exploratory fields of surgery. I tried to follow the examples of these renowned, much-admired, medical risk-takers, all of whom had an impact on my development. And, in turn, I taught younger surgeons who stood at my side in the wards or in the operating room, hoping that they would be as bold and as determined as the surgeons who taught me.

In the early days, treatment for tuberculosis was very conservative, with little medical intervention per se. The patient received a great deal of sun, a change in diet, and plenty of rest. If the lung was not stuck to the chest wall, a pneumothorax procedure was performed. This allowed the lung to collapse and gave it a chance to heal. For very advanced cases, thoracoplasty was performed in which a number of ribs were taken out so that the lung could be compressed by the soft tissues of the chest wall. Treatment of the disease improved significantly with the addition of streptomycin. This was the first antibiotic that had any real impact on tuberculosis. However, until a variation of the drug was developed, an unfortunate occasional complication of streptomycin was the onset of deafness. Another drawback of the drug was the fact that it could only be given to the patient by means of a painful intramuscular injection.

As time went by, newer drugs became available, as well as combinations of drugs that were more effective. Surgery for pulmonary tuberculosis also changed from being primarily palliative to being more radically curative and treatment-oriented. Sometimes, we would remove a diseased lung or lobes of a lung, if the disease had spread too invasively. We also treated tubercular meningitis. Occasionally I would have to open a skull to insert a catheter into the brain to facilitate a necessary injection of streptomycin.

I assisted Radford with all these procedures, an opportunity not given to most surgeons; it made me competent to perform complicated surgeries inside the chest. Radford also had me do the routine general surgery that arose in the population of 2,000 patients at King George V Hospital.

Dr. A. G. Sweetapple, one of the senior surgeons attached to King George V Hospital, resented my presence at the hospital and made very public noises to that effect. The superintendent of the hospital, however, Dr. Bill Dormer, took steps to ensure that my position was secure. He advertised the position of general surgeon and then personally travelled to Pretoria, where the selection was to be made, to ensure that the right person was chosen. Needless to say, I won the competition. I held the position of general surgeon at King George V Hospital for some thirty years, from 1955 until I retired in 1985. My duties at King George brought me to the hospital approximately once a week to run a clinic. I was also available for consultations.

My private practice kept growing and around 1980, I decided to curtail it somewhat. I had been at it for more than thirty-five years and it was time to make a change. With the approval of my partners, I took time off from the practice for three or four months of the year.

Lola and I decided to travel. We established a home in Haifa where my brothers Hymie and Havis lived. Lola's sister Adeline (Addy) lived not too far away in Ramat Hasharon, just north of Tel Aviv. She was married to Syd Cohen, a doctor, but also a distinguished pilot and commanding officer in Israel's air force during the War of Independence. We would stay in our home in Haifa for three months and then visit Toronto where Mike and David lived, then return home to Durban.

I always said I would stop operating at the age of sixty-five. I am quite certain, in the way that hindsight and retrospect allow us to be fearlessly certain in our judgments, that I could have carried on until seventy-five. But I did not want to persist in the work, as I saw so many others do, to the point when my abilities started to decline. So on April 1, 1985, I retired from practice, although I still maintained some contact with my colleagues and my patients for five more years as a consultant.

To announce my decision, I sent out the following notice to all my colleagues:

A time comes to us all, and I think this is my time, so with mixed feelings I have decided to retire from operating after a stint of thirty-two years as a surgeon. However, I will be available for consultations and will still continue to follow up all my post-operative cases. May I take this opportunity to thank you for your loyal support over the years.

Yours sincerely,

M. Stein

*"Mannie's reputation was that of a leading general surgeon
in Durban, highly respected by his colleagues and patients and
feared for the high standard he demanded from his nursing staff.
The theatre staff, where Mannie was "king" of his domain,
were sure to give of their very best while the maestro
was at work.*

*"...Mannie was an icon for any surgical attention required by
the members of the Jewish community of Durban, in particular,
but his reputation extended far beyond those confines.*

*"Mannie's retirement from his surgical practice and his departure
for Israel and then Toronto, was a loss for Durban;
and it is a gain for Toronto to have Mannie and his wonderfully
courageous lady, Lola, as citizens."*

—SYLVIA AND CYRIL KAPLAN, JULY 2001

CHAPTER 13 | **Israel**

I GREW UP IN A HOME with a very strong Jewish identity. Judaism, Israel, Zionism were all of a piece. The millennial Jewish dream of returning to Zion was a central tenet of the faith that was practised in our home. My father was a devout man who never compromised on the details of his observance. In the 1930s and especially after the war in the 1940s, new details were added to the daily ritual of his observance and his devotion. They were the details of the Jewish struggle unfolding in the faraway cities and hillsides of mandated Palestine.

In our house, indeed in most Jewish households in South Africa and undoubtedly throughout the entire Diaspora as well, we were all focused on the future of the Zionist enterprise. The events of World War II lent urgency and a sense of desperate poignancy to the need to establish an independent, sovereign Jewish state. Supporting the establishment of such a state formed part of the core of our identity as Jews and as individuals. Thus, from our earliest days in Zionist youth movements in South Africa, Israel played a very large role in our lives. Our attachment to the young country would forever be unshakable.

When the United Nations General Assembly voted to partition British-mandated Palestine into a Jewish state and an Arab state, Lola and I were in Dublin. Anticipation of the vote was electric. The entire community was alive with a fervour that was a mixture of tears, happiness, foreboding, and faith. The atmosphere was charged with excitement and an unmistakable air of history in the making. The Jews of Dublin felt an additional measure of pride in the occasion because the former chief rabbi of its community, Rabbi Isaac Halevy Herzog, was now the chief Ashkenazi rabbi in Israel. One of his sons, Chaim, whom I met later in Israel, would one day become the president of Israel, after a long and distinguished career in the Israeli Defense Forces (IDF) and as ambassador of the Jewish state to the United Nations. His other son, Yaakov, a brilliant scholar and diplomat, served as Israeli ambassador to Canada in the early 1970s, but died at a young age in mid-career.

After the results of the vote were announced, Lola and I joined in the large and festive community celebration. Religious and non-religious people alike felt the tugging of this special occasion. We all knew beyond a doubt that we were sharing in a unique moment of Jewish history. How memorable and moving and emotional it was: singing, dancing, and drinking. For a few brief hours of that unforgettable evening, we set aside our concerns and worries for the safety and well-being of the *yishuv* (the Jewish community of Palestine). We were all following the reports of the attacks by local Arab gangs and occasional forays of the irregular army formations from neighbouring countries that had already begun. But the intensity of our celebration did not abate. We seized the moment to affirm, along with our fellow Jews, that the Return to Zion would soon evolve from dream to reality.

In 1959, eleven years after our celebration in Dublin, Lola and I made our first visit to Israel. We both had family there and we wanted to visit them as well as the young Jewish state. Subsequently, each time we travelled, we stopped in Israel. During the early years of our visits to Israel, we would stay in Haifa with Havis and his wife, Leila and then in Ramat Hasharon with Lola's sister Addy and her husband, Syd. After a number of years, however, when we could better afford it, we stayed in hotels rather than with our respective siblings. It was more private for us and for them too. I'm sure they preferred it as much as we did.

At one time, I toyed with the idea of settling in Israel. I was asked to open a vascular unit in Haifa by a senior surgeon who had come from Jerusalem to start the cardiology unit there. After devoting a great deal of thought to the matter, I decided against it. At that stage in my life, I felt it was simply too much of an undertaking and too much of an imposition on my family, though I felt I could have settled in Israel and lived there quite easily had I done so earlier in my life. Our regular visits there came as much from our love for the country as from our love for our family.

In the late 1970s, on Havis's advice, we bought a piece of property in Dania, a suburb of Haifa. We bought three plots of land, each of which was one-and-a-half *dunam* (quarter acre) in size. I owned one plot, my friend owned another, and the three of us, including Havis, owned the third plot. After a while we sold the third plot, dividing the profits three ways. I kept my property for many years. We built a large home of about 325 square metres on the property, with Havis supervising the construction. It was finished in late 1981. After our home in Dania was built, we increased the length of our annual stays in Israel to about three months. As I have said, my partners in Durban gave their blessings to the arrangement that allowed me the luxury of being away from the practice for three months of the year. In fact, even while I was in Israel I still received my share of the income from our medical practice.

Of course, each time we visited Israel we got to know more and more of the country. We never tired of our visits. We travelled its length and breadth, visiting communities in the Upper Galilee, staying in the comfortable but rather sparse guest houses of Kfar Blum, where my brother Hymie had lived, to the more lavish and luxurious hotels in Eilat on the shores of the Gulf of Aqaba.

126

Our home in Dania was a very happy place. It was large enough to accommodate generous numbers of guests, and it often did.

Pesach, it seemed, was the time when large numbers of us—family and friends—came together. The seder, after all, was the occasion for such gatherings. The first truly memorable seder that I recall in Israel took place before we owned our Dania home, in the Tadmor Hotel in Herzliya. Havis's family was there, as were some of Leila's four siblings who lived in Israel and Lola's sister Addy, her husband, Syd, and their family.

The seder was held in our own very large private room. The numbers of children and adults lent the occasion an air of happy *balagan* (chaos). But no one seemed to mind. We delighted in the occasion and in the fact that we were together, celebrating the significant springtime festival in a lovely hotel on the seashore in Israel. We were served by two waiters and a maitre d'. Because it was Israel, and they were Jewish too, and we could not bear the thought that they were missing their own family seder, we asked them to take part in our seder. We invited them to read portions from the Haggadah, which they did in their turns, in flawless Hebrew, of course. I do not believe we could have felt that special feeling of community and festivity anywhere but in that special land.

Our first seder in our home in Dania was in 1982. It, too, was a wonderful, happy, boisterous gathering of friends and family. As usual, Havis and Leila joined us from Haifa and Syd and Addy from Ramat Hasharon. But this time, Freddy Davidson from England and Harry Fine and his family from Jerusalem also joined us. Lola prepared the bulk of the food for the seder but, as is the custom in Israel, everyone brought something to the table. We sat up quite late into the night. When we finished telling the story of the Exodus, we found other stories to tell as well.

Another very special Pesach I recall was in 1996 when a very large assembly of friends and family met in the Princess Hotel in Eilat where we held a double celebration: the holiday and the seventieth birthday of our dear friend, Morris Schaffer. Many of our mutual friends travelled all the way from South Africa to be in Eilat for that special Pesach. It seemed our Pesach that year was one prolonged but very joyful holiday.

The fact that so many of our friends from South Africa joined us in Eilat, was, and is, typical of the circle of men and women with whom we grew up and spent most of our time. Loyalties among our friends ran very deep. No effort was ever spared when comradeship or assistance or support was required on behalf of a member of our circle. We made it our business to share as much as we possibly could in one another's personal and family milestones. Thus, it was not unusual for an entire troupe of colleagues to travel so far away from home to be at a friend's bar mitzvah.

I was not in Israel during the Six-Day War. Like most Diaspora Jews, however, I meticulously and fearfully followed every detail of the news. The story is a familiar one to most of us. For weeks leading up to the war, there was a state of great anxiety throughout the country. The Straits of Tiran had been closed to Israeli shipping. The UN forces had withdrawn. Egyptian troops were massed in the Sinai. The neighbouring Arab countries were expressing increasingly hostile sentiments toward Israel. And yet, inexplicably, the government of Prime Minister Levi Eshkol seemed uncertain of its course. Eshkol himself seemed only to add to the level of national doubt by his slow and cumbersome deliberations. When the clamour among the people for a unity government became too much for him, Levi acquiesced, creating a national unity cabinet and appointing Moshe Dayan as minister of defense. This immediately lifted the country's spirits. The people were anxious to break out of the noose they felt tightening around them with each passing day. Break out they did, in a manner that history will record as one of the most brilliant campaigns of self-defence ever fought.

When the war was imminent, Havis was called up to his military reserve unit. Hymie, by then, was too old to be called up. Havis was attached to an armoured corps unit that provided support to front-line tanks. His unit moved quickly through the West Bank and then headed north to the Golan. He tells the story of his unit rolling through Merom, in the Galilee, on Shabbat. As they moved through the town, they were met by scores of observant Jews who had come out of their houses and onto the streets to feed the arriving soldiers. The townsfolk brought out their cookware and portable stoves, started boiling tea, cooking food, making all sorts of other foodstuffs and feeding the weary soldiers. It was Shabbat! The sun had already fallen below the western horizon. And all along the main street, the townsfolk, most of whom were observant, were labouring over various instruments of cooking to provide food and nourishment to Havis's unit of soldiers. Havis was deeply moved by this tender outpouring of affection and responsibility. Even as he recollected the incident for me, many years later, he had tears in his eyes.

After their short rest in Merom, Havis's unit regrouped at Tsomet Golani and sat waiting for further instructions and for any pieces of information on the course of the war. None of them had any idea where they were headed next. Havis happened to be outside the command tent when he overheard the orders: *Kadima. Anachnu zazim.* Forward. We are moving.

They left on the Friday night. Havis had half a bottle of brandy with him and made a promise to his friend that if they get to the top of the Golan Heights alive, they would finish the bottle of brandy then and there. They reached the summit of the Golan Heights and came into the city of Kuneitra. It had been completely evacuated by the Syrians when they arrived. It was the only time in his life that, at 9:00 in the morning, he drank half a bottle of brandy.

Six years later, when the Yom Kippur War broke out, Havis was no longer fit for service, having had his chest opened three years earlier with the discovery of his tuberculosis.

Lola and I were in Israel in 1973 when Israel was attacked on Yom Kippur. I was sitting in synagogue with Havis and another friend who was closely connected with the army. Suddenly, a siren went off and we could hear cars moving around quickly on the streets outside. It was bizarre and very unsettling to hear those sounds on Yom Kippur. We knew instantly, as did everyone else, that something was terribly wrong.

The news of war spread like wildfire. Even though there was a blackout on all news, pieces of information filtered through. The Egyptians had attacked across the Suez Canal and caught the IDF off guard. At the same time, the Syrians had attacked on the Golan Heights. The borders had been penetrated. Jordan, thank God, had not joined the fighting except for a symbolic movement of some of its forces.

At the outset of the war, the Israeli military forces were in a dire predicament. But after three days, the situation began to change and more news concerning the course of the fighting started coming out. The Egyptians had been halted in the south. The IDF had regrouped in the north and was able to regain the initiative against Syrian forces. In the first fateful hours of the war, when the northern border was defended by only a hand-ful of soldiers, the Syrians had managed to descend the Golan Heights and had reached into the Galilee. Had they continued their progress, they could have cut the country in half. But they stopped their push down from the heights in mid-success—no one knows why.

After sixteen days of fighting, the Israelis again succeeded in throwing the Syrians out of the Golan Heights and were themselves parked a few kilometres from Damascus. The Egyptian army was completely surrounded in the Sinai desert and the IDF was on the western side of the Suez. The Americans and the United Nations demanded a ceasefire, and so the war ended. Given the point from which Israeli forces had to rally after the initial three days of onslaught, the victory in the Yom Kippur War was, arguably, more spectacular than that of the Six-Day War. But it came at a horribly high price. More than 2,000 soldiers were killed and thousands more wounded, injured, and scarred for life.

During the war, I volunteered my medical services and was attached to the Surgical Department of the Beilinson Hospital in Petach Tikvah. This allowed the regular hospital staff more time to tend to military casualties. I also volunteered to accompany an air force aide whose melancholy task it was to bring the sorrowful news to the homes of fallen pilots from Ramat Hasharon that their husband or father or son had been killed in action. It seemed an important piece of work to be at the aide's side, to try to help console someone during what was, essentially, an inconsolable situation. At times I felt the consolation and comfort was as much for the lonely aide as it was for the grieving family.

When civilian travel returned to normal, some days after the war's end, Lola and I returned to Durban.

Over the course of my many visits to Israel I became friends with many of the senior people in the upper echelons of the medical establishment there, including all the heads of the departments at the Rambam Hospital in Haifa. I also knew Chaim Sheba quite well. Sheba, of course, was one of the giants of Israeli medicine. Israel's largest hospital, at Tel Hashomer in Tel Aviv, is named after him. Whenever I went to Israel I would visit Tel Hashomer Hospital and go on the wards with him to see, at first hand, the nature of patient care there and the advancements that took place from year to year. Chaim and I became good friends, so much so that, in subsequent years, when Mike went to live in Israel, Chaim said to him, "You must look upon me as your father in Israel."

Due primarily to my connection with my brother-in-law, Syd Cohen, I was also able to meet many of the senior people in the upper echelon of Israeli life, such as Moshe Dayan, Moti Hod, and Ezer Weizman. Because of Syd's prominence in the early days of the Israel Air Force, his circle of friends included some of the more distinguished names in the military elite. And, of course, in Israel, the military elite often also evolved into the political elite. Syd had been Ezer's commanding officer in the War of Independence and they became close friends.

In 1988, three years after I retired from surgery in South Africa and just before Lola and I made our permanent move to Canada, we sold our home in Dania. Subsequent visits to Israel were as tourists to the hotels.

Our last trip to Israel was in 1990. After that, Lola's condition was not conducive to long-distance travel.

"How do you say 'thank-you' to someone who has saved your life? Now that the initial shock is over, I am back to my normal, happy, smiling self for which both my husband and I will be eternally grateful to you."
—JEAN LEVY, JUNE 1977

CHAPTER 14 | **Havis**

I AM VERY PROUD of all my brothers.

During our youth, as young brothers first in Vilkomir and then in Durban, we were as close as siblings could be. Morris, my older brother was actually born in Stalingrad (Tsaritsen, as it was known in imperial days). Hymie and I were born in Baulnik—he, on the eve of our departure for South Africa. Havis was born in 1930 when our family was already well-settled in Durban, some four years after we had landed.

As we grew older, however, it was inevitable that we would also grow somewhat apart. I left home at the age of sixteen for medical school and returned only periodically for short stays at a time. I was away, therefore, for the critical, beginning stages of my brothers' adult lives. They finished their schooling, chose their livelihoods, found their mates during the time that I was away from Durban. And, of course, like most other siblings, we were very different in temperament as well as in interests.

Thus, we mapped out distinct paths for ourselves.

Morris was the biggest and toughest of the brothers, my protector in grade school. He was an adept athlete, which, when coupled with his size, won him the position of goalie for the field hockey team at university. He remained in Durban and became a successful small businessman.

Morris was a Revisionist in his politics towards Israel. Havis, Hymie, and I—although neither Hymie nor I as passionately as Havis—were Habonim socialists. You can imagine the discussions and the arguments around the table at home when we were all together. There were strong political arguments all the time. But we would all come together in the end. There was never any lasting residue or bitterness or resentment from our arguments.

The festivals, especially, were always warm occasions in our house. Large numbers of family members and guests would congregate there. *Leil seder Pesach* (the night of the Passover seder) was always a big event in the Stein household.

Morris died very suddenly in 1986. I received an urgent phone call in the evening from my sister-in-law to come right over. They had just finished dinner. Morris had gone to lie down because he wasn't feeling well. Not more than ten minutes had passed from the time I received the phone call to my arrival at their home, but it was already too late. When I stepped through the door, he was already dead.

He and his wife, Miriam, raised five daughters: Sandra studied pharmacy and now lives in the San Diego area, Michelle, a computer scientist, lives in Israel; Marsha, Dalya, and Batya all live in Toronto—Marsha trained as a child psychologist; Dalya, as a town planner; and Batya as a lawyer.

Haim was the smallest and the slimmest of the brothers. He completed his matriculation, started a stationery business, and did very well. Then he undertook a radical change of course. Soon after the war, he went with a group of *chalutzim* (pioneers) to Kfar Blum, a kibbutz in the Upper Galilee. Along with his young comrades, he did the backbreaking work of clearing the land and draining the mosquito-infested swamps of the Hula Valley. Unfortunately, he contracted meningitis. He became very ill and went back to South Africa to recuperate. Indeed, my mother travelled to Kfar Blum to bring him back to Durban. Soon enough, Hymie recovered from his illness, restarted his business, and got married to Joyce Den.

But a home and a life in Durban were not what Hymie wanted. He was determined to return to Israel. And so he did. He and Joyce settled in Haifa, where Hymie built up a successful insurance business, and raised two sons, Julian and Michael. Unfortunately, Hymie's adult life was marred by illness. He required surgery to repair an aneurysm of the aorta. Some years later, at a relatively young age, he died of a heart attack.

Although they never explicitly spoke about it, it was obvious that my parents were very proud of the fact that two of their children—Haim and Havis—had settled in Israel.

Havis was always bigger and stouter than I and far more outgoing. His gregariousness was a quality that served him well as the chairman of the debating society at Durban Boys' High School.

We were always very close. Perhaps it was because I, literally, saw him being born. Perhaps it was because the ten-year-age difference between us kept our relationship free of the typical sibling rivalries and jealousies that are normal in all children who are close in age. Havis's deeply embedded sense of right and wrong was cultivated early in his life and was part of the deep motivation, I believe, that inspired him to join the *chalutz* movement. He decided at an early age that he would live in Israel. It is no overstatement to say that a large part of his youth was devoted to helping prepare himself to fulfill that decision.

Havis moved to Israel in 1955, when he was twenty-five years old. His life in Israel was one of important public service and significant achievement.

The formative part of his life in South Africa was spent in the Habonim youth movement. It played a major role in his life and he was strongly indoctrinated into the progressive, collectivist Zionist philosophy of this group. Havis attended his first

Habonim camp when he was only five years old. His attendance at that camp was actually a condition my parents imposed on Hymie and me in order to allow us to go to the camp. One could almost say that Havis became the mascot at the camp that year. Subsequently, of course, he went to many, many Habonim camps. Eventually, he took charge of the Habonim movement in the province of Natal. In 1952, he was asked to run the movement in Johannesburg for one year.

In the Habonim youth movement, many of the comrades frowned upon the idea of going to university. The goal was to become *chalutzim*, pioneers capable of working with one's hands, of doing something of practical benefit to the people and to the nascent country. This left Havis with a dilemma, for he had a fine, academically inclined mind and had always done well at school. He was headed for university. He wanted it—and our parents expected it. So, in typical Havis fashion, pragmatic and wise, he found a compromise that would let him pursue his studies, remain true to his movement's principles and save face with his Habonim colleagues. He enrolled in the Faculty of Engineering at Natal University.

Havis maintains that he did not have any inclination to actually work in the field of engineering. It just seemed to be the best and most practical way out of his dilemma. At that time in South Africa engineering was not a particularly Jewish calling. Out of 120 students in his first-year engineering class, there were only three Jews. The other two were from South West Africa (later Namibia) and Egypt.

If he had to choose again, he says he would choose law. Nonetheless, Israel was destined to receive a young Stein civil engineer not a lawyer. To this day, Havis says that his university studies were a sideline. His main activities were with Habonim which, according to him, was "also a good way to meet girls."

In fact, Havis first met his wife, Leila, at a Habonim camp in Cape Town in 1946. They met again some months later at a national Habonim camp attended by some eight hundred people where they started up a more serious relationship. But camp was camp. Havis went home to Durban; Leila went home to Cape Town.

Leila's father, Moshe Baruch Morgenstern, was the most respected rabbi in South Africa. Local rabbis always sought out his advice. Leila's mother also came from a famous rabbinic family in Lithuania, the Atlas family. They were wonderful people.

To be sure, Habonim was not anti-religious, but it was certainly not pro-religious either. The norm was to be non-religious. Havis followed the norm. Moreover, there was a Marxist basis for many of the lectures and programs in Habonim. But Havis's non-religious way of life never adversely affected his relationship with Leila's parents.

At his wedding, Havis delivered his speech entirely in Yiddish. It was somewhat uncommon for our generation in South Africa, but he did so as a tribute to our parents and his parents-in-law. It was a great testament to the character of Leila's parents that the non-religious lifestyle that Havis and Leila chose was never an issue for them and that they never made it an issue for Havis and Leila.

Havis's father-in-law died in South Africa at a relatively young age and his mother-in-law eventually settled in Israel.

In the late 1940s, Havis required my professional help for a certain medical situation. He was playing with a penknife one day and almost severed his little finger. It was hanging by a thread. I took him to my colleague, A. A. Sweetapple, who tried to join the two parts of the finger together. After some time, he felt that the procedure was not properly taking hold and suggested that the nearly severed portion of the finger be snipped off. I asked him if I could take over Havis's case, which, of course, Sweetapple did not mind. I re-attached the tip of the finger and within two weeks the two parts of the finger were knitting together perfectly.

I subsequently sent Havis a bill for 100 guineas (a guinea was one pound and one shilling). In return, Havis sent me a cheque for thruppence! I never cashed it.

It was also around this time that I was called in to deal with another "situation" involving Havis. He had been working on our mother to buy him a motorcycle. She, of course, was having a hard time refusing the youngest of her children and was inclined to get him his motorbike. To me, though, the mere idea seemed foolish and risky. I do not recall if she asked my advice, but I gave it freely anyway. I prevailed upon her to revoke her decision.

"Why not buy the boy a motorbike?" I calmly, yet sarcastically, suggested to my mother. "Of course, you should buy Havis a motorcycle if you want to give him his death certificate."

Well, that was the end of Havis's campaign to enlist my mother's help in acquiring a motorcycle. She refused to go along for the ride, so to speak. But, as in all things, Havis was relentless. Eventually, he did get his motorcycle. But it was much later and he paid for it by himself, without any contribution from our parents.

At the end of 1951, the movement sent him on a six-week leadership training program to Israel. In 1952 he became the head of Habonim in Johannesburg. In 1953 he came back from Johannesburg to Durban. He was still associated with Habonim, but more in an advisory capacity. He was no longer an active leader. A new generation had moved up the ranks.

With a bit more time on his hands, he began working for the city engineer's department. Havis had decided that at least a little bit of experience and money would be beneficial before he made *aliyah* (moved to Israel).

In 1954, Leila visited Durban. She and Havis renewed their relationship. They were married in January 1955 and made aliyah the next month.

In those days there was no shortage of work for engineers in Israel. Havis's first job was with the Ministry of Agriculture in the soil conservation department. The mere idea of helping to conserve the soil of Israel appealed to him a great deal.

His first undertaking was an irrigation project at Tabgha on the northern shore of the Sea of Galilee, near the church of Capernaum, which was, according to Christian tradition, the site of the miracle of the loaves and fishes. The heat was unbearable and the mosquitoes were plague-like. After the Tabgha project, he worked on another irrigation project in the western Galilee. The work was always interesting, but difficult. He would be in the field each morning by about 5:00 a.m., return about 10:00 because after that it was simply too hot to stay outside, then go out again about 4:00 in the afternoon. Even in the field, he was part of the ingathering of exiles for the *chevreh* (group of comrades), who, along with him, consisted of Iraqi and Moroccan Jews. Here, in the hot fields of the Galilee alongside his clutch of new friends, he learned his Hebrew.

Havis has often remarked that an exciting and inspiring spirit blew across the young country then. Everybody felt they were doing something worthwhile to help build a unique society. Young people from all over the world, inspired and determined to contribute to the rebuilding of the Jewish homeland the way Havis and Leila were, flocked to Israel. Indeed Havis and Leila lived in a community with other young people from virtually every continent on the globe—from the US, Canada, South Africa, South America, Holland. The place throbbed with youthful energy and dynamism. The challenges Israel faced were many, but there were none too great nor insurmountable for the cadre of young people who had made Israel their home and whose confidence in their own skills soared to a level as high as the belief in the justice of their cause.

After three years with the soil conservation department of the ministry of agriculture, Havis became the district engineer for drainage in the Hula Valley in the Upper Galilee. He was now working for the Israel Water Planning company, TAHAL, as it was known by its acronym for *Tichnun Hamayim L'Yisrael*. TAHAL was a government-appointed company, charged with designing a national water system for the country. Havis's office was in the then-new community of Kiryat Shmoneh, but he often slept in Metullah, the northernmost settlement in Israel. When he went into the field, he carried an Uzi submachine gun and a revolver. The weapons were necessary because of the frequency of attacks by marauding Arabs from the nearby borders with Syria and Lebanon.

Havis's first two jobs in Israel would have brought a smile to some of the founding fathers of the Zionist movement, men such as A. D. Gordon and Achad Ha'am, whose singular messages spoke of the reclamation of the soul of the Jewish people through the reclamation of the soil of the Jewish land. Bringing water to the parched earth and removing water from the swampy earth were the first two assignments Havis took on in the lofty experiment of the Zionist challenge. In both he richly succeeded.

It was around this time, in 1959, that Lola and I made our first visit to Israel and, of course, to Havis and Leila. They were living in Haifa even though Havis was stationed in the Galilee. Their apartment was tiny and on the third floor of the building. I mention the floor because of the crystal-clear memory I still have of a man who carried a refrigerator up the three floors to Havis's apartment on his back.

Our first visit to the country lasted about a week. Havis had his own Jeep and his own Uzi, of course. With Havis as our guide, we travelled from the upper Galilee to the lower Negev. The experience was exhilarating and exhausting. We slept very little. But it hardly mattered for we were swept along by the freshness, the dynamism, the beauty, the novelty, and the excitement of what we were seeing. It would be the first of our many trips back to Israel.

One of the very many pleasing memories I have of my frequent visits with Havis is of our occasional sorties to the Balfour Cellar restaurant in Haifa to enjoy their *cholent* and *kishka,* a delightful gastronomic experience for two men reared in the culinary traditions of eastern-European cholesterol festivals. *Gribones* were harder to find. Unfortunately, that restaurant no longer exists.

Havis soon looked for new challenges in the task of building the country. He found one with a construction company owned by a fellow South African, a Cape Towner, Paul Goldschmidt. Eventually he became chief engineer of the company. He worked for Goldschmidt for ten years, from 1959 to 1969, building many projects in both the public and private sector. In fact, they built the first high-rise—a twenty-four-storey structure—in Haifa.

The lingua franca on the building sites in those days was Yiddish. Havis employed a basic crew comprising twenty-five permanent workers, of whom two were Arabs. All the specialized trades work was subcontracted out. One of the quaint, even lovely traditions in the construction business in those early days was to celebrate the completion of the construction of the roof of a structure by having a roof "wetting," a party on the roof after it had been finished. Refreshments were provided for the workers, a few short self-congratulatory speeches made and then a *l'chaim* drunk by all. The wetting was to give expression to the, no doubt, very gratifying feeling of having achieved something together. That feeling, especially in that time and place, was worthy of a celebration.

In 1969, Havis again changed jobs. He returned to TAHAL to run its office in Nigeria. At that time, TAHAL was designing water systems in fourteen different developing countries. Under the auspices of the Foreign Ministry, Israel had devised a brilliant form of foreign aid. Lacking the means to provide financial assistance to needy Third World countries, Israel instead provided a commodity that it had in great abundance: scientific know-how and a creative, innovative approach to agrarian and hydrologic matters.

Israel had developed a large roster of experts in water and other agricultural-related fields. It was an innovative, constructive, meaningful, virtually perfect form of assistance for the many countries that were now also acquiring their independence from colonial rule in Africa and other parts of the world. Israel was looked upon by many emerging countries as a model of self-reliance and the pioneering spirit.

Israelis were welcomed to the developing world as friends and teachers. Unfortunately, this particular form of foreign aid came to a halt after the Yom Kippur War. The realpolitik of the Cold War, the overbearing diktats of oil diplomacy, and the resulting oil embargo "persuaded" many African nations, who had benefited so tangibly and meaningfully from Israeli foreign aid, to sever diplomatic ties with the Jewish state.

Thus, Havis moved his family to Ibadan. His responsibilities there were a combination of administration, diplomacy, and professional engineering work. He had a full-time Israeli assistant, a full-time Nigerian engineer who had studied at the

Technion in Haifa, along with a permanent team of Nigerians to whom they taught land surveying. Together, they supervised the actual construction of the various projects.

TAHAL designed and supervised the development of diverse distribution schemes that brought water to some twenty million people in Nigeria. By the time Havis arrived in Ibadan, the large Israeli contingent had already dwindled. In its heyday, there were more than a hundred Israeli children at the Israeli-run school there. When Havis's children attended, there were only twenty.

Havis was in Nigeria at the time of the Biafra civil war. A curfew was in place. No one could go out at night. He thus had to be careful, as well as innovative, in the work he performed on Israel's behalf. One of the major projects Havis procured for TAHAL, despite stiff competition from American, German, and British firms, was the rebuilding of the destroyed water distribution system in eastern Nigeria.

Havis quickly learned that dealing with government officials in the competition for business always entailed a certain amount of diplomacy or negotiations particularly when competing with American, British, French, and German organizations.

Havis was also asked by the Israeli government to go to Ghana and Liberia to try to drum up more work for TAHAL, resulting in partial success. After a year and a half, Havis and the family left Nigeria. When he returned to Israel at the end of 1970, he was offered and accepted a post that would lead to the position of TAHAL's vice-president for international business.

A week or ten days after Havis began his new job, he became seriously ill with a respiratory illness that no one seemed able to properly diagnose. After a long stretch of uncertainty, the doctors decided to open up his chest to have a look.

After surgery, the doctor said to the anxious family, "I am happy to tell you that Havis has TB." Everyone had feared that

Havis had developed cancer. It was, therefore, an enormous relief to be told that Havis's illness was "only" tuberculosis. Lola and I were in Israel when Havis was hospitalized. I remember that I left Israel at that time, in 1970, not knowing whether I would ever see my brother again. But the illness was not cancer. Havis recovered and we have seen each other often and a great deal since. Though the illness was not a threat to his life, it did mean that Havis could not take the job as the vice-president of TAHAL.

After his recovery from tuberculosis, Havis took up sailing. He is now a full-fledged skipper.

In 1972, Havis left TAHAL and opened Stein Engineering Services, an office for management and supervision of civil engineering works. In the mid-1980s, during the period of the high inflation rates, Havis undertook another change in career. He became an arbitrator.

The last project that Havis worked on was Tayelet Louis, the Louis Promenade, in Haifa. Paul Goldschmidt asked Havis to oversee construction of the project that was built and named in memory of Goldschmidt's son who was killed in a motor accident. Havis's name and that of the architect appear on a plaque on the Tayelet, which was finished in 1990. Havis's days of reclaiming and irrigating soil, distributing water, and supervising construction projects have long since passed. These days he takes things much easier. His two children, Yoav and Dina, have also been very successful. Yoav was awarded a doctorate at Yale in the field of computer science and is now a professor at Stanford University in California. Dina received her doctorate from Hebrew University and is a professor of Rabbinics and Folklore at the University of California in Berkeley.

"Mannie was one of that lost breed of general surgeons who could and would tackle almost any problem that came his way. In the beginning he made his name for treating peptic ulcers by doing gastrectomies and the various modifications that developed therefrom. Much later, he was one of the first to perform vascular operations for abdominal aneurysms, a technique he perfected. The next step was to do vascular grafts for obstructed vessels. At all times, he was a very efficient operator, never looked as if he was in a hurry, but completed the job in a shorter time than average.

"He used to start operating at 7.30 a.m. and he meant 7.30. He was there already, scrubbed up and starting. If I was the least bit late in arriving in time to assist he would be halfway through the job, or if it was an appendectomy, the offending organ was already in a dish on the table! He was a stern, disciplined operator and the staff loved him and feared him…

"In the wards he was much loved and respected. The chief surgical ward was always known as Mr. Stein's ward and the nursing was kept up to a high standard. I know that he was much missed when he left, and he is remembered with much reverence…

"He made it his interest to be concerned about the whole Durban community and he was fondly nick-named 'The Godfather,' so much so, that people who had ailments totally unrelated to his specialty, would not do anything until they had his opinion."

—HYMIE BERKOWITZ, MAY 2001

CHAPTER 15 | **Syd**

I FIRST MET SYD COHEN when he was a medical student in Johannesburg and courting my wife's young sister, Adeline (Addy). Apparently, Addy had often spoken to Syd about Lola and me. She wanted us to meet. One day, when there was a major international rugby match being played in Durban, they got into Syd's car, travelled to Durban, knocked on our door, and came for a visit.

I must have seemed rather strange to Syd when we met. I was reading a book when they arrived. I got up from my easy chair, introduced myself, said hello, and returned to the chair. The two sisters went into the kitchen and Syd was left in the living room, with me, so to speak, but on his own. I don't recall that I said another word to Syd. He must have felt rather awkward sitting in the same room with me, being completely ignored. In retrospect, it seems a bit rude on my part, but I certainly intended no discourtesy. I was simply engrossed in my book. He must have arrived at a critical moment in the plot! In truth, however, I cannot imagine Syd Cohen feeling awkward in any situation. He was a large, imposing, six-foot-two-inch bear of a man. He was a handsome, dashing figure who, depending upon his expression or the way the sun shone in his eyes, resembled either Ernest Hemingway or Clark Gable.

I knew very little about him then, other than that my sister-in-law liked him—and I presumed he liked her as well. I knew that he was studying medicine and that he had fought in World War II. Over the years, of course, I would learn a great deal about him. He and I would become like brothers—best of friends and confidants.

Syd Cohen was born in 1921, one year after I was, in Bothaville, a small Boer farming community in the Free State province of South Africa. There were only fifteen Jewish families in Bothaville, but they still managed to support a syangogue there. Syd was one of seven children. His parents were born in Lithuania, but had moved to England with their respective families. They married in Scotland and, in 1916, emigrated to South Africa where Syd's uncle—his father's brother—was living. The frequent movements of Jewish families from eastern Europe at or near the beginning of the last century says a great deal about the economic hardships they endured and the lengths to which they would go to provide some measure of stability—economic and, most likely, physical as well—for their families. The Cohens' move to South Africa was to be their last move. Like so many other immigrant families in those days, Syd's father arrived in South Africa first and then summoned his wife and children. My mother travelled to South Africa with three young children in tow. Syd's mother was "carrying" four—Syd and two of his siblings were born in the new country.

Many years later, I operated on Syd's father, who was suffering from colorectal cancer. Syd told me that his father said of my work that I had *goldeneh hent* (golden hands).

Having been raised in the countryside, Syd's childhood was a far cry from that of city dwellers like my brothers and me. Apart from the Yiddish he heard spoken in his home, Syd's first spoken language was Afrikaans; English came afterward. But even though they did not live in the big city, his parents ensured he received a Jewish education. Until his bar mitzvah, Syd attended cheder every day after school.

His first job after he graduated from high school was some 8,000 feet below ground in a gold mine. When World War II broke out, he was working in a dynamite factory. He wanted to enlist in the war effort like oldest brother, who was already serving in an armoured car corps. But all the employees of the dynamite factory were exempted from conscription because the government deemed them to be working in a key industry. That exemption "pissed him off no end," as Syd colourfully explained. So he decided to remove himself from the key industry and enlist anyway.

In 1940, Syd found his way to the South Africa Air Force recruitment office and enlisted there. In 1941 he received his pilot's wings, having learned to fly on the venerable Tiger Moth and Hawker Hart airplanes. In those days, Syd sported a large, bushy beard and was often called the flying rabbi. The very next month after Syd received his wings he was sent on active duty to Cairo. Syd remembered the moment when he received his fly-boy wings as one of the proudest moments of his life.

All four Cohen brothers served in South Africa's armed forces. His oldest brother, Morris, was in the tank corps and was wounded in the battle of El Alamein. His brother George was a pilot too; in fact, he got his wings before Syd did. Tragically, he was shot down by anti-aircraft fire about a month before the battle at El Alamein, in a sortie against a German airfield. Although two crewmen survived, George was killed along with one of his gunners. His brother Isaac also served in the air force, as part of the ground crew.

Syd saw his first action in the skies over the northwestern desert of Africa. He was part of a South African wing formation serving in the Royal British Air Force, piloting P-40 Tomahawks and then the P-40 Kittyhawks. He had only been an active pilot for a short time, with fewer than 160 hours of flying experience, when he had his first dogfight encounter with enemy Messerschmitts. With good luck and good skill he survived that encounter. Messerschmitts flew higher and faster

The first board of directors of the Workmen's Accident and Rehabilitation Centre in Durban, 1966. (I'm standing, far right.) I was one of a group of three doctors who persuaded the Commission for Workmen's Compensation to start this centre.

Four generations of females in the family, 1980: Lola, our daughter, Linda, two of Linda's children, Lara and Tanya, and Lola's mother, Freda Jankelson.

Our daughter, Linda, with her second husband, Tony Berman, taken in our garden at 491 Essenwood Road, Durban, 1980.

Our son, Mike, and his wife, Pam Medjuck, at their wedding in Halifax, Nova Scotia, 1988.

Our son David's marriage to Jana Skrha. Under the chupah, Lola is giving Jana the wine to drink. The wedding was held on Mike's farm in Caledon, Ontario, 1989.

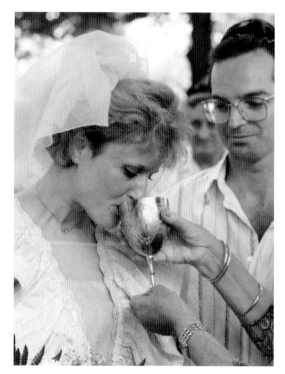

Our children, Mike, Linda, and David, at David's wedding.

With Lola and our three children, David, Mike, and Linda, on the occasion of my 65th birthday, 1985. Mike's presence was a complete surprise. He had flown from Toronto to Durban to be at my birthday. The party, too, was a surprise.

Lola, between her two sisters, Annette and Adeline, at our golden wedding anniversary party, held in Toronto in October 1995.

Lola, still lovely as ever, at our golden wedding anniversary.

Making a speech at our golden wedding anniversary. In the foreground is my very close friend, Morris Schaffer.

Returning to my roots, 1997: Mike and me in Balninkai, Lithuania, where I was born.

With Lola, our granddaughter, Lara, and her husband, Mark, at their wedding, June 2001. Though extremely ill, Lola made a supreme effort to be at the wedding. Lara especially made the wedding in Toronto so Lola could attend, even though it meant the family had to come from South Africa. Lola passed away three months later.

My 80th birthday at our home in Toronto, April 2000: Lola and me with our twelve grandchildren, as well as Kim, wife of my grandson, Warren.

than the heavier Tomahawks and they constantly sat in wait for them, swooping down upon slower British aircraft like lethal predators.

In November 1942, Syd found himself in Egypt with two of his brothers, Morris and George. Deciding to visit Palestine, the brothers toured every corner of the tiny country and soon fell in love with it. They were especially taken with the kibbutz system that they encountered at Ein Charod, where they spent a great deal of time. The three Jewish brothers in uniform must have cut an unusually dashing figure, for, as Syd recalls, everyone "made a very big fuss over them." Their visit lasted a month and left a favourable impression on all of them. For Syd, that visit laid the emotional foundation for the role he would soon undertake in trying to protect the very existence of the nascent Jewish state.

After the Tunisian and El Alamein campaigns, when the war in North Africa had essentially come to an end, Syd was sent back to South Africa to be an instructor in an operational training school for fighter pilots. By then he already served some fifteen months as a pilot and had taken part in 135 different missions.

His duties as a fighter pilot instructor lasted only until the middle of 1944, when he was sent to Europe, to be based in Italy. He fought there until the war ended, piloting Spitfires attacking enemy forward lines, disrupting communications installations of the enemy, or supporting advancing Allied troops. When the war in Europe came to an end, Syd volunteered to serve on in the Far East. His boat had made it as far as Ceylon when the atomic bombs were dropped on Japan, bringing to an end all the hostilities of World War II.

After the war Syd went back home to South Africa to study medicine at the University of Witwatersrand in Johannesburg.

But he could not concentrate fully on his studies. He was pre-occupied by his experiences in the war, his visit to the *yishuv*, and the memories of the friends on Kibbutz Ein Charod. He dutifully listened to the BBC and read as many accounts as he could to stay abreast of events in Palestine.

It was not a great surprise that he decided to put his medical studies—already in progress in his third year—on hold and to volunteer to help the Jews in Palestine. The Zionist Federation of South Africa had organized a group of such volunteers and, at the suggestion of Boris Senior, Syd joined them. Israel needed pilots. Syd had been a pilot in the South African Air Force and was now ready to be one for the new country of Israel.

His route back to the *yishuv* was a circuitous one. He would have to go through Czechoslovakia. Ironically, he was told that he was needed there to learn how to fly Messerschmitts! He thought it absurd that his first call of duty was to learn to fly the plane he had spent half his military life fighting. But in June 1948, Syd wound up at the Budejovice Airfield in Czechoslovakia. To get there he had had to stop in Nairobi, Khartoum, Libya, Malta, Rome, Geneva, and Zurich.

Along with Syd in Czechoslovakia were a number of other veteran volunteers recruited for the new air force of the Jewish state. They all would soon become Syd's mates at the air force base in Israel. After a month's training, Syd and his comrades flew to Israel in a transport plane, inside of which was a disassembled Messerschmitt and various pieces of ammunition.

Incidentally, Syd did not like the Messerschmitt. He said it was not a very easy plane to fly. One problem with the Messerschmitt was that the guns fired through the propeller and there was trouble with the timing mechanism. On one run, Syd came back with three blades of his propeller partially shot away. The exact reason for this remains unclear. Some of the pilots felt that the

Czechoslovakian mechanics might have deliberately misfit the mechanism. Whatever the reason, the problem was eventually solved.

It was now July 1948 and Israel was fighting for its life in what would later be called its War of Independence.

Syd immediately joined the sole fighter squadron: 101 Squadron. Its air base had recently been moved from Ekron to Herzliya. The runways of the airstrip were shoddy, but there was not much that could be done about it. The new recruits didn't really even know how the war was going. Most of them spoke very poor Hebrew; indeed English was more or less the language of the base, with generous smatterings of Yiddish. The pilots and other air force personnel had come from all over the world, but they seemed to be predominantly English-speakers: Canadians, Americans, British, and South Africans. The commander of the base was an Israeli named Mordechai (Modi) Alon. He was much younger than most of the pilots, but enjoyed wide respect among them. In that entire first fighter squadron there were only three Israelis: their commander, Modi Alon, Ezer Weizman, and Sandy Jacobs. Jacobs had qualified as a lawyer at Oxford and all the Americans and Canadians called him "Little Oxford" because he had a lovely, refined accent.

In August, the squad received its first Spitfires in disassembled parts that had been stored in different locations throughout the country.

One month later, however, Syd and some of his colleagues were called upon to participate in a historic mission: to fly fully assembled Spitfires into Israel, for the very first time. Israel had managed to buy a number of Spitfires from the Czechs and the planes needed to be flown over to Israel. Syd took part in the operation with five others: Sam Pomerantz, Modi Alon,

Boris Senior, Jack Cohen, and Tuksi Blau. To prepare for this mission, dubbed "Operation Velveeta," they headed back to Czechoslovakia.

The pilots took off from Zatovice in their newly adapted Spitfires. The planes had been made lighter and were also outfitted to carry extra fuel tanks. The flight back to Israel called for a stop at a secret base in Yugoslavia and, in all, the flight lasted about nine and a half hours. Of the six planes that left Czechoslovakia, only three arrived in Israel. Blau crash-landed in Yugoslavia; his plane was unusable afterward. Alon and Senior had to emergency land in Rhodes because they were low on fuel. They spent a month in prison there and their planes were lost as well. Jack Cohen, also from South Africa, Sam Pomerantz, and Syd made it safely to the base in Israel. That flight from Yugoslavia to Israel was the longest distance that the Spitfire had ever flown.

A VIP reception was waiting in Ramat David for the young pilots and for the first ever Spitfires to be owned by the Israeli Air Force. Unfortunately, although the ground crews had made sophisticated adjustments and adaptations to the planes to enable them to fly so great a distance, they forgot to make any adjustment to the planes' equipment that would enable the pilots to relieve themselves while travelling for so long a time across so great a distance. Syd was the first pilot to land and remembers that the very important first item of business for him was to empty his bladder. As he approached the runway, he saw a long line of cars with a great many VIPs waiting to greet the first Spitfire ever to land in Israel. When he got out of the plane, everybody started to walk toward him. He immediately put up his hand and said, "*Rega echad*"—wait a minute. Then he turned his back on the approaching crowd, faced toward the airplane, and "peed for about fifteen minutes."

On the second Operation Velveeta, four more Spitfires were brought to Israel. But Sam Pomerantz was killed when his plane crashed into a mountain. Eventually Israel moved about thirty planes out of Czechoslovakia.

One of Syd's colleagues, Leo Nomis, described an encounter with Syd just as Syd was departing for a reconnaissance mission:

"When I come out of the operational tent, Syd is going by in a Jeep with the squadron operations officer. They stop and I ride out to the Spitfire dispersal point with them. Syd is going on a photo reconnaissance flight to Gaza and, as he puts on his gear, I tell him about the *shuftikite* (enemy spy plane) episode. He laughs and goes over and looks at the map which Croll, the squadron operations officer, seems to eternally have in his hand. A Messerschmitt is taking off and we can't hear anything for a minute. Syd wipes his mouth with his forearm. When he gets up on the wing of the Spitfire, Croll extends a revolver in a fabric holster toward him. He tells Croll he doesn't want it. He says they are too bulky to wear in the cockpit and that they are too dangerous to be carrying if you are captured. Croll agrees but says it is an order from headquarters that the reconnaissance pilots must wear a sidearm. Syd still doesn't want it. Croll looks at the ground beside the wing for a moment. He says it's not necessarily for use against the enemy. He says it's for Syd to use on himself if he is captured by irregulars. The statement amuses Syd. He takes the gun and straps it on and climbs into the cockpit."

Some weeks after the first Operation Velveeta, in mid-October, the commander of 101 Squadron, Modi Alon, was killed in a crash-landing when returning to base. His wife, who was pregnant at the time, happened to be on the base and watched in horror as her husband's plane crashed. Alon's death was a tremendous loss to the squadron and to the still-forming air force. He was regarded by all as a fine individual and a fine commander who knew how to handle his men.

That night, Syd was called to the office of the commander of the air force, General Aharon Remez, and asked to assume command of the squadron. He accepted. One observer from those days wrote about the decision that "Air HQ chose the experienced and greatly respected Syd Cohen to take over Alon's mantle, and he would lead the squadron throughout the rest of the war."

Syd Antin, one of the pilots in 101 Squadron, like many, was impressed with Syd's leadership: "Syd Cohen was a great guy. Everybody loved him. He commanded a great deal of respect. He had a great deal of wisdom for his age and experience and people respected that."

In November 1948, the squadron moved to a more southerly base, in Castina, to be closer to the Egyptian front. On March 14, 1949, with the war nearing its end, Syd had the honour of directing the ceremony at which the IDF Chief of Staff, Yaakov Dori, gave out the first ever Israel Air Force pilots' wings to new graduates. His last air action was five days after the ceremony, on March 19, in Operation Abraham.

A few weeks later, at the end of March 1949, just after the IDF captured Eilat, and the war was virtually over, Syd handed over command of the squadron to Ezer Weizman. Syd would recall that Weizman was a good pilot, but that he could also be a bit of a wild guy. For example, Ezer was the squadron's chief *ganev*, or scrounger. There were so many transport shortages in those days that when anyone in the squad needed to find a vehicle, they turned to Ezer. He found them everything they needed—Jeeps, buses, cars. The police seemed to turn a blind eye to the "used car lot" that was known to exist at 101 Squadron.

Syd returned to South Africa to complete his medical studies. He also resumed his relationship with Addy and some months later, in 1949, they married. In 1952 he graduated from medicine and set up his medical practice, first in a mining town and then in Durban. They lived near our house and we, of course, helped them become part of Durban society.

Although Syd had left Israel, Israel never left him. In 1963, he and Addy went back for a short visit. He met with many of his old colleagues and friends, and the desire to live there returned. He and Addy decided to make aliyah. Two years later, in 1965, they moved for the last time and settled in Neveh Rom, the pilots' neighbourhood in Ramat Hasharon. Syd had doctor's privileges at Tel Hashomer Hospital and ran a clinic out of his home. He also became a doctor for the air force.

The adjustment to Israeli life was not easy, though. In fact, it was quite difficult. Syd received encouragement from a great many different people. He tells a story that, one day in 1965, Ezer Weizman took him to see David Ben-Gurion. Ben-Gurion's wife, Paula, was apparently very attentive to the way Weizman was eating and constantly urged him in her distinctive American accent, "Weizman, drink; Weizman, eat!"

It was very gratifying to Syd that Ben-Gurion remembered him from the days, some seventeen years before, when he had been at the head of 101 Squadron. The Old Man, as Ben-Gurion was known, asked Syd how he was getting along. Syd answered honestly that it was a bit more difficult than it had been in 1948. Ben-Gurion did not hesitate for an instant and answered with equal honesty. "I don't like what's going on in South Africa. You will have to get used to life here now!" He did not have to elaborate.

After that meeting, Syd's integration into Israeli life seemed to go more smoothly.

In the Six-Day War and in the Yom Kippur War, Syd was doctor on many air force missions. Through his work and through his friendships with some of the air force establishment, Syd knew most of Israel's political leaders and distinguished people in Israeli society. In 2000, Syd retired as the chief medical officer for El Al.

Syd was and is a true hero. He understood the significant and awesome events unfolding before him. He understood, too, that he had to take part in them, that if great events in world history are to be steered towards a better, more just resolution, individuals must become involved and place their hands on the wheel.

Syd's exploits in 101 Squadron are recounted in *On Eagle's Wings*, Ezer Weizman's autobiography, and in the book *No Margin for Error* by Ehud Yonay. There is also a web site dedicated to 101 Squadron, in which all the details of the squadron's founding, its members, and their operations are retold with admirable detail and reliability.

"We both want you to know of our deep gratitude and thanks for your skill, dedication, and constant care and concern during my recent operation. Had it not been for these outstanding qualities, which have so rightly earned you the praises of all who know you, 'things' would have been a lot different for both of us, we know."
—TED AND DOLLY COTTIER, NOVEMBER 1979

CHAPTER 16 | **Lola**

I SAID AT THE VERY BEGINNING of this book that I am not readily given to sweeping statements of large emotion. While I have always been an appreciative person, I have not generally been an elaborately expressive one. My mind has generally responded to the calibrations of science and mathematics rather than to the tuggings and stirrings of poetry and song. But I knew fairly quickly and fairly suddenly after I saw her that Lola was the woman for me.

As I have described, we met in Pretoria while Lola was working in Tryza, a local pharmacy. I was on a locum. In subsequent years I found out that she had also liked me from that first encounter. She may even have embellished the extent of that instant attraction by telling some of her friends that Mannie "swept me off my feet." There was no doubting, however, that she was a happy woman. She was clearly pleased with her profession. It showed in her ever-smiling countenance and polite, positive disposition. She was sensible, reasonable, bright, fun to be with, and so very attractive. Light seemed to shine from her.

Lola must have had an interesting childhood. She was born in Butterworth, Transkei, one of three sisters, the daughters of Moses and Freda Jankelson. Her father was born in Lithuania and came to South Africa in his early adolescence. Her parents settled originally in Oudtshoorn, where they ran an ostrich farm. But when the market for ostrich feathers collapsed, they moved to Butterworth. After a few years in Butterworth, they moved to Pretoria. Lola grew up in Pretoria, studied pharmacy, and had the distinction of becoming one of the first women to graduate in pharmacy there.

Our courtship was not long, but it was intense. Even after my locum ended, I would drive from Johannesburg to Pretoria and return the same day—just to be with her. After she graduated, I asked her to marry me. Oh, how nervous Lola was before she met my parents! My father did not speak English very well—they mostly spoke Yiddish. And Lola did not know any Yiddish. How would they take to her, she fretted. Of course, while Lola stewed in her agitated state of nerves, I was rather amused by it. I knew my parents and I knew Lola. The match was as perfect for them as it was for me.

As I have already mentioned, we were married in October 1945, in a double ceremony with her sister Annette, lived with my parents for about two months after the wedding, and then left for England to start my postgraduate studies. The move to Durban and then from Durban to Europe was a precursor of a way of life that required Lola to move households many times, with all the disruption on the family that numerous resettlements involved.

Wherever we made our home, however, it was always a perfect reflection of Lola's personality—full of grace and charm and elegance. She loved to entertain and was so very good at it. She was a natural hostess, primarily because she loved people. She had an instinctive aesthetic sense around flowers and an uncanny ability, it seemed, to evoke from any arrangement or bouquet the most splendid splashes of colour and fragrance.

Despite, or more accurately, on account of my successful career, Lola did not have an easy life. She had to cope with a husband who was at work day and night. She essentially raised the children by herself. She took them to their programs, activities, dances, music, plays, and games, essentially by herself. I hardly saw the children when they were young. She took care of them.

But even as I reflect on our lives from this vantage point, after so many years have passed, I do not know if I could have done it differently. I do not believe I could have been the very best doctor I wanted to be, and needed to be, had I practised medicine any other way.

But, alas, there was a price to pay, which both Lola and I paid in our different ways.

In later life, unfortunately, Lola experienced increasingly deteriorating health. But, like the flowers she would arrange in a vase, she handled it all with grace and dignity. The pain, constant medication, machines, wheelchair confinement, diminishing strength and vigour—in spite of all her suffering and travail, she was never self-pitying or morose. She always greeted others with a smile.

The story of Lola's illnesses began many years ago with the chronic back trouble of sciatica. She even underwent surgery on her spine, but the pain did not completely go away. To relieve the pain, she took tablets called APC that contained aspirin, phenacetin, and caffeine—or codeine, in stronger tablets. Unbeknownst to any of us at the time, the phenacetin was destroying her kidneys. But we did not appreciate the harm the drug was causing. Over the years, she took a great many of those tablets. Phenacetin has since then been banned.

Because Lola also suffered from ischemic heart disease, we rejected the option of kidney transplant for her. In retrospect, this may have been the wrong decision, for it meant that she had to continue with the hemodialysis, which began in 1992, for the rest of her life.

Her kidney function gradually deteriorated until she reached a stage that required dialysis. In the early 1990s, doctors tried peritoneal dialysis—in which a little tube is inserted through the tummy. But something went wrong and the abdominal area became septic. Lola had become septicemic. Fluid built up in her chest cavity and she nearly died. She was in the hospital for a long time.

While Lola was in the hospital, a situation arose in which I had to force the hand of her doctors. I noticed that she had developed a high temperature, had become confused, and even irrational. One night I felt her tummy and I could feel the swelling of an abscess. I called the doctor. The hour was well past midnight. The junior resident appeared.

Pointing to the abscess on Lola's stomach, I told the doctor, "This has got to be opened." The resident left the room to consult with her chief. She returned shortly, but said the procedure would be scheduled for tomorrow. I argued that the situation was urgent and could not wait until the next day. Pressing the case further, I told the doctor, "If you don't open the abscess, I will, right here on the bed."

The doctor left to call her chief once again. The chief must have told the resident to open the abscess right there in the ward room because she returned and cut it open; out came about 3 litres of pus. The next morning Lola felt much better. The infection had drained. But the original kidney problem still remained. After she recovered from that stormy passage, the doctors decided to start hemodialysis.

At first, they tried to create a shunt. They joined an artery and a vein so that the size of the vein would be enhanced, making it easier to find the vein. That didn't work well. They then put in a graft from a vein into the artery. That worked for a while. Eventually, however, that opening closed up as well. The doctors then put in another graft. They took a plastic tube and joined a vein onto an artery in the shape of a "U." This created a larger area that could be punctured from time to time. That worked for about three or four years. Then it too blocked up completely. Lola's doctors then put in another graft that lasted for approximately five years, a straight graft down from the armpit. But that graft also became blocked from time to time and had to be de-clotted. The doctor cleaned out the graft and dilated it back up a number of times. Eventually, the graft had narrowed so much at the top end that the doctors had to put a stent in to keep it open.

Lola was dialyzed three times a week, which essentially took up three full days. I was always with her. At first the dialysis was performed at the Toronto General Hospital. Then it shifted to a local self-care dialysis centre. Finally, the dialysis was done at home every Tuesday, Thursday, and Saturday. At one point, Lola was trained to do her own dialysis. On those days, we got up early. I would set up the machinery and the equipment for her, which took about 45 minutes. The nurse would come and do the dialysis for her.

But Lola's mobility did not become so restricted in the later years because of the dialysis. In June of 1999, Lola fell while walking into the clinic. She broke her femur and injured her knee joint. Somehow, it never healed well and infection set in. Had she been younger, we could have tried more aggressive treatment. Some years earlier, in South Africa, Lola had had a hip replaced due to the onset of arthritis. Unfortunately, in 1995, she dislocated the same hip and it had to be replaced again. They operated on the femur, put in a new plate and screws. She did quite well with that, but it took her a long time to recover. By then, Lola was walking with the aid of a walker. But she went to the rehab centre at the Toronto General and, with the walker, was quite independent.

To add to her misery, however, at around the same time, Lola needed a cardio-angioplasty with the insertion of a stent for angina. One day at dialysis, Lola's blood pressure fell drastically to 80 systolic. She was normally hypertensive at 160 to 170. Since the reading persisted, she was admitted to hospital. While in the hospital she started to fibrillate. Her heart rate became irregular and rapid. She stayed in the hospital for quite a while. The doctors could not quite pin down the source of Lola's new problem. They conducted every investigation under the sun. One of the senior staff members said he thought the result of the MRI on the spine showed the presence of a secondary tumour there, which had spread from somewhere else.

I thought to myself that this is not the picture of a secondary cancer. It just would not present like this. A secondary cancer in a bone will usually come from the thyroid or from the kidney; it might even come from the lung. In men, it can come from the prostate. But Lola's situation did not fit the template.

I phoned the doctor who used to clear the clog in her grafts and asked him to recommend an expert in interpreting MRIs on bones. He was able to get his expert to look at Lola's MRI and he concluded that hers was a normal MRI, but with a normal bone cyst.

If I had not continued to hover over Lola and assess the measures being taken by her doctors, they would have likely said, based on an erroneous diagnosis of cancer, that there was no point in doing anything more for her. They would have probably just let her go. But, with the proper diagnosis and appropriate course of treatment, Lola gradually improved, until once again some bad luck intervened.

Lola had been prescribed the medication Zocor. Occasionally, but not often, Zocor can cause the complication of paralyzing muscle. Unfortunately for Lola, she was affected by the drug in this way. She became so weak, so paralyzed, that she could not lift her head off the pillow; she could not lift up a cup of tea. None of her doctors realized what was happening to her until she was examined by rheumatology experts at the Toronto General. She was immediately taken off the drug. The upper body recovered fully; the lower body, unfortunately, did not.

She could not walk. We tried desperately to get her to walk. Then, the prosthesis, the part of the artificial hip that goes down the femur broke through the bone. Lola had become so osteoporotic, her bones had become so thin, so friable, that she was in constant risk of harm. The plate that was on her femur had pulled away from the bone. If we were to remove the plate and the screws, the likelihood was that her bones would crumble. In that event we would have to amputate her leg. We knew she would not want that.

After consulting with my good friend Cyril Kaplan, an orthopedic surgeon at the Montefiore Hospital in New York, we decided to simply leave the status quo. Lola's situation was so extreme, it could not sustain surgery. At one point, while sitting in her chair, Lola tried to retrieve something from behind her and she felt a sharp pain. I am certain it was a tear in a ligament of the right shoulder. After that the heart fibrillation started up again.

In the later years of her life, Lola's health story was one of seemingly unending suffering, pain, and bad luck.

As Lola's life closed in on her more and more, I tried never to leave her side. While she had at least the walker-assisted mobility, we could still travel to our family and friends. I could put her in the car and we would go out at night for a visit somewhere. But even that became impossible after the refracture of her leg. She was confined to her chair and, basically, stuck in front of the television. I grieved for the fact that she was unable to get outside, to breathe the fresh air, to look up at the sky from outside.

In an irony that awakens the sleepy heart, I became mindful that over the last decade, I dedicated my attention to the details of Lola's life and to tangible expressions of my love for her in ways that the schedule of a busy vascular surgeon in Durban had not allowed. Lola's physical and emotional well-being and comfort became my highest priority.

On dialysis day, for example, I got up at 7:00 in the morning to prepare the dialysis machine for the nurse, which meant getting the machine ready and sterilizing, cleaning and connecting the dialysate and tubing. The nurse came to the house at 8:30 to put in the needles.

I carefully watched Lola's medication, checked her heart and pulse and consulted with the family physician on a regular basis. Like all people with kidney ailments, Lola was frequently tired because her hemoglobin count was lower than the norm. To assist her in her breathing, we acquired a nebulizer, a machine that mixed a solution and created a mist that Lola could breathe in. She also had an oxygen machine nearby in case she needed it. Every few hours, Lola had to be turned in bed or needed to receive medication. I tended to all her needs.

As she had, for almost fifty years, tended to my needs and to those of our family with her smile, her serenity, and her grace.

❖ ❖ ❖

On October 1, 2001, Lola passed away. It was the saddest, hardest day of my life.

*"Your contribution to the people of South Africa and
to the people of Durban in particular have been enormous and
you richly deserve the great esteem in which you are held.
For myself, I have no hesitation in saying that you were
the best surgeon I ever met, both in South Africa and the UK."*
—Freddie Davidson, April 1985

CHAPTER 17 | **Family and friends**

Our family home in Durban was a welcoming sanctuary for friends, family, and, especially, for me, when I returned each night and, more than occasionally, a number of times a day, from the hospital or some other place where I was required for a medical emergency or a meeting or a consultation.

It was a grand, lovely home, with a wide surrounding garden that offered up for Lola's brilliant, almost metaphysical affinity for floral arrangements a seemingly unending supply of purple bougainvillea and myriad other bright pink and orange flowers. The long driveway was always cluttered with bicycles and other paraphernalia that belonged to our children and, in turn, to our grandchildren. The front yard accommodated a large, square swimming pool, which was very well-used, especially in the hot and humid summers that were a feature of Durban's tropical climate.

The interior and, I would add, the character of our home were a reflection of Lola—a font of hospitality, always warm, full of light and sun, dignified, elegant, and a fun place to be. Not surprisingly, therefore, it was a very busy place. People were always visiting, or dropping by. At the dinner table on Shabbat there were almost always fifteen to twenty people. And around the pool on Sunday, we always had a barbecue. So many happy memories revolve around that home.

But, of course, as the line of one's life cuts through more and more years, some of the memories will also be more complex, some quite sad.

One of the worst memories I have is the memory of my

mother's death. She died in 1956, at a young age, still only in her sixties. I was only thirty-six and still too young to be mourning the loss of a mother. Over a short period of time, she became quite ill; she had a carcinoma of the rectum. The doctors operated to remove the cancer and, at the same time, they removed a large ovarian cyst as well. But complications set in and she died post-operatively in December 1956. She had never recovered from the operation.

Some time after my mother passed away, my father married an Israeli woman around his age. The decision was momentous enough for him that he felt the need to consult with the rabbi before doing so. The rabbi, of course, cleared my father's conscience. We never resented his second wife—indeed, we were quite pleased with her. Not long after they married, my father suffered a stroke and his new wife was a godsend to him—and, it must be said, to us too. She looked after my father until he died in 1963.

Six years after my father died, Lola's father passed away. Then, twenty-six years later, in 1995, Lola's mother, the last of our parents, passed away.

Thankfully, to some extent, our three children knew their grandparents, although, David, our youngest child was just an infant when my mother passed away the same year he was born. It meant a great deal to us that the children had been able to be with and develop a rapport with their grandparents. Indeed, I often wondered how successful Lola and I were at conveying to our children some of the positive, strength-giving residue of what we may have received from our parents.

Our daughter Linda was a beautiful young girl who always caught everyone's eye. Unfortunately, her parents could not protect her from the trauma and sadness that entered her life at a relatively early stage.

Linda studied social sciences at Cape Town University. In her final year, on one of her trips back to school, she was involved in a horrific car accident. Her car went over a cliff. She actually fractured her spine. But it wasn't an ordinary compression fracture; it was a transverse fracture. Miraculously, somehow, she managed to climb up the cliff, flag down a motorist, and get to the hospital in Cape Town.

Lola and I were on our way home from Israel when the accident happened. As we landed in Johannesburg, a message from my partner Roy Wise awaited us, informing us of the situation. We decided on the spot to travel immediately to Cape Town and flew straight down to be with her.

Linda was ordered to stay in bed for three months. We arranged for a Red Cross plane to fly her back to Durban. The Secretary of Health personally intervened to send us the plane. Although I did not know him, he quickly responded to my personal call for assistance. We were deeply grateful for his swift response and kindness.

Cyril Kaplan met us at the Durban airport and took us straight to the hospital. When Linda was released from the hospital, she remained in bed for the entire second semester of university. After her convalescence, she returned to Cape Town, wrote her final exams, and passed them.

Not too many years later, Linda would have to further rely on the strength of character her accident instilled in her to get her through an even more unimaginable hardship. Linda's husband, Anthony Schewitz, passed away from lymphoma. It was only about two years from diagnosis of the disease to his death. Facilities for the type of treatment Anthony needed were not available in East London where they lived. As a result, he went to Cape Town for treatment. I visited him in the hospital each weekend in Cape Town, flying there on Friday and staying with him until Sunday. It was a strenuous time for me, indeed for all of us, but how could I not be with my son-in-law and daughter?

After Anthony died, their children—Lara, nine years old, Warren, seven years old, and Tanya, eighteen months old—came to live with us in Durban. Eventually, we found an apartment for Linda and the children not far from us. Tanya never really knew her father. To a great extent, she was raised in our home. Two years later Linda remarried. Her new husband, Tony Berman, was a widower with two young children of his own, Lance and Kelly. Linda and Tony were ideally suited for each other and all the children meshed well from the very beginning. Their combined, reconstituted home of five children was a happy one.

Mike, our second child, was always quiet and introverted, but also independent-minded and full of initiative. When he was thirteen, he bought plans for a sailboat and built it in our garage in Durban. He bought the timber, the fibreglass, the rigging, and all the necessary material, assembling the entire boat piece by piece from the frame of the hull up. On his own, he even found somebody with a workshop and a lathe so that he could form all the metal fittings. Finally, he bought the sails and the boat was ready for the water and for competition.

Mike and a friend entered the national regatta with that boat and won. It was quite an accomplishment, quite a feat. It taught me, and him too, I imagine, a great deal about Mike's self-reliance and determination.

A little while after his victory in the national regatta, I took him along on one of my medical trips to Europe. It was in the mid-1960s; he was, as I have said, thirteen years old. This was the time I went to Amsterdam to observe Dr. Boerema's work on the use of hyperbaric chambers in the recovery of surgery patients. While I spent the entire day with Boerema, Mike travelled up and down the Amsterdam canals, arranging his entire day's touring and travelling by himself!

It was on that same trip that we went to Glasgow to see Professor Illingworth, the author of one of the pathology textbooks that we had used in medical school. He was very accommodating and helpful to me. I spent the entire day with him, returning to the hotel at night.

"What did you do today, Mike?" I asked my young travelling companion when I settled back into the hotel room.

"I took a trip to see the castle in Edinburgh," Mike answered.

By himself, he had toured Scotland that day. This was a precursor of the resolve and resilience that Mike would show in later life. When he lived in Israel, for example, he took on whatever jobs became available to support himself, however backbreaking and arduous they were, such as carrying meat carcasses into cold storage or trawling for fish off the coast of Haifa.

Once, when he was backpacking in Spain, the police locked him up because they did not like his scruffy appearance. He kept his cool, showed them his traveller's cheques and his passport and demanded to see his consular representative. When the commanding officer returned from his lunch, he quickly released Mike. The impressive detail from the whole unpleasant incident was the way Mike handled the situation, staying calm and composed even though he was all alone.

When he finished high school in December 1968, Mike went straight to Israel. Within a week he was gone. We all agreed to his decision because it was evident that he simply could not make his peace with apartheid. He wanted no part of such a society. He enrolled at the Technion in Haifa to upgrade his Hebrew and math before entering into the engineering program. In his first year of engineering, he was allowed to write his exams in English. In the following years, he wrote them in Hebrew.

After graduating with an engineering degree from the Technion, Mike then moved to Montreal to study for an MBA at McGill. Six months later, Lola and I met him in New York and suggested he continue his MBA studies at Columbia. He was accepted at Columbia and finished the MBA program there in thirteen months. I think these unique personality traits and these facets of character underlie the great success Mike has achieved in his career.

David, our youngest child, studied chemical engineering at Natal University in Durban. After his degree he moved to Canada and worked as a chemical engineer in the Northern Ontario town of Hearst. He worked on a special project to develop a system of converting sawdust into a gas that could be used in timber-cutting equipment to cut more timber that would in turn generate the sawdust to convert into gas, and so on. The letters he sent us from Hearst told us of an entirely different world and way of life than that which we lived in Durban. For example, in the winter it was so cold that he could not spend more than five minutes at a time outside.

David worked in Hearst for about a year and then also headed to New York to get his MBA at NYU. After his MBA, he returned to Ontario—this time to Toronto—and started a business in property development.

Both our boys were now engineers with MBAs. The combined breadth of a scientific and business education would serve them very well in the months and years ahead. They were ethical entrepreneurs with driving, intellectual, and sharply inquisitive minds, who believed in one another, trusted each other totally, and enjoyed working together. Not long after the collapse of the Soviet Union, they realized the far-reaching business implications of an entire semi-continent changing from a tightly controlled state-run economy to a free-market economy.

The boys went to Eastern Europe to explore "the lay of the land" and the business opportunities there. After a great deal of research, they decided to open a lens factory in Prague and David moved there to oversee the enterprise. He now directs the company from his home in France. The start-up of the factory was characteristic of the boys. It was a totally new initiative. Neither Mike nor David had any prior experience in manufacturing, let alone in manufacturing and marketing reading-glass lenses. Neither of them had any prior experience doing business in Eastern Europe. Mike was a civil engineer. David was a chemical engineer. Yet David was not deterred. He persisted. He persevered. He runs the business all by himself and it is very successful.

❖ ❖ ❖

It was a natural decision, although not without tears, for us to emigrate to Canada.

At the time, both Mike and David lived in Toronto and we had been frequent visitors. We knew the place, quite liked it, and felt comfortable and at home. We had no difficulty in getting landed immigrant status as we were sponsored by our children.

Our departure from Durban was very hard for Linda, as it was for Lola. In truth, it was also hard on me. Even though many of our friends had left South Africa by then, many also remained. Still, it was the only home that Lola had ever known, and it had been my home for all but six years of my life. But we resisted the inertia of remaining and felt that we should make the move while we were still physically able to do so without the additional burden of weakness or infirmity. Moreover, we intensely disliked the politics in South Africa and had grown increasingly ill at ease in so harsh a world, where society was defined by its divisions.

Emigration is not easy at the best of times. Not surprisingly, therefore, even though we were not the proverbial strangers in a strange land, it still took us some time to get used to our newly permanent surroundings, to arrange all the formalities and documentation for our health care, driving licences, and other needs. Fortunately, accommodation was not a problem. We moved into an apartment that Mike owned on the lakefront. For the first four years, we avoided the Canadian winters by spending the months between October and March in Durban. Lola had to carry the extra burden of maintaining—for a time—three homes: in South Africa, in Israel, and in Canada.

We landed in Canada in March 1988, just before Pesach, and headed straight to Halifax where Mike was about to marry Pam Medjuck. Pam was born and raised in Halifax. The Medjuck family was firmly established in the Maritimes, widely known, indeed, almost part of the folklore of the area. The Steins of Durban, on the other hand, were an unknown commodity. The bride's side knew nothing about us: neither our background nor our history. Though most of the speeches at the wedding were for the Medjuck family, our many friends and family who travelled great distances—from South Africa, Israel, and the US—to attend the wedding spoke on behalf of the Stein family. I spoke extemporaneously at the wedding and made reference to the fact that we were celebrating on *Shabbat Hagadol*. Lola declined the invitation to speak. She disliked public speaking and recoiled at the mere thought of having to stand up before a gathering of people to make a presentation. It was an elaborate, festive affair and laden with great symbolism for us. We had uprooted ourselves from the land we knew in South Africa to join in the unfolding of our children's lives, now taking root in Canada. There could be no more poignant symbol of the new rooting of the Stein family than this wedding.

After the wedding, we headed to Toronto to establish our own home in Canada.

A year later, in the summer of 1989, David married Jana Skrha. Jana had defected to Canada from Czechoslovakia some years earlier while she was an air hostess for the Czechoslovakian airlines. One day, after landing in Montreal, she managed, by stealth and great courage, to get on a flight to Vancouver, where she hid from the Czech authorities. She managed to support herself with odd jobs while taking various courses in bookkeeping, interior design, and computers. She soon became a Canadian citizen.

David and Jana met in Toronto and were married on a small farm Mike owned in Caledon, north of Toronto. It was a wonderful outdoor affair arranged by Mike and Pam. Again we were joined by family and friends from South Africa, Israel, and the US, as well as by Jana's parents and sister from Prague. David and Jana bought a house in the Toronto district known as Cabbagetown, gutted it, and renovated the house completely. In 1995, David and Jana moved their family first to the Czech Republic and ultimately to the south of France.

During the summer of 1989, Lola and I moved into a condominium in mid-town Toronto. We then made plans to sell our homes in Israel and South Africa. In the early 1990s Lola was already on dialysis. It was unrealistic to expect we could any longer maintain three homes. It was simply too onerous an arrangement. After 1992, we did not return to South Africa. Lola was not well enough to do so.

Our home in Toronto was well-suited to us and well-situated. An entirely modern facility with exercise and entertainment facilities, centrally located, it is set in a green, verdant neighbourhood surrounded by trees and parks. Most important of all, however, it is very close to Mike and Pam and their children.

Our grandchildren have always been one of the sweet, sustaining pillars of our lives, enabling us to reach ever upward into a higher level of emotion, joy, happiness, and satisfaction. Linda's children are, of course, the eldest. She married at a much earlier age than either Mike or David. As I have said, she and Tony have five children: Lara, Lance, Warren, Kelly, and Tanya. As I write these words, they are all adults, talented, creative, bright, and successful in their respective fields. Like many people, however, who are originally from South Africa, they are today flung far across the face of the globe. Lara, who married Mark Myerson in the summer of 2001, lives in Singapore; Lance and Kelly live in New York; Warren, who married Kim Myerson in December 1999, lives in Toronto; and Tanya, who married Marc Sternberg, lives in Cape Town.

As anyone who has ever worked with me can attest, I was generally a strict, disciplined person. When my own children were young, I tended to act in the same way at home—not always sufficiently, lovingly expressive. But I was different with my grandchildren. Perhaps it was simply the fact that I was older, more experienced, wiser, and somewhat gentler in my approach to people in general. Perhaps it was Anthony Schewitz's death.

At any rate, I made a point of being far more physically affectionate with my grandchildren than I had been with my own children. I hugged them a great deal. I smiled at them a great deal. I tried to ensure that when one of the youngsters walked into the house, they were received with a big smile. To this day Warren tells the story that I taught him how to drink Scotch by sneaking him a drink when his mother was not looking; and that Lola taught him to gamble by slipping him a few rand to play on the horses when I was not looking! Our friends, such as Morris and Judy Schaffer, Gerald and Hilary Hackner, Reggie Berkovitz, and Jonathan Beare, a gregarious, fun-loving, close-knit group, were also a big part of the youngsters' lives. Our home was a busy place. And the children saw it all and took part in it all. When they reached the age of their bar or bat mitzvahs, Lola and I took them to Israel. Though we could not shelter them from all harm, Lola and I did try to ensure, as much as we could, that our grandchildren's lives would be infused with love, affection, opportunity, and happiness.

Mike and Pam's children—Jason, Matthew, Liane, and Eva Rose—are much younger than Linda's. So too are David and Jana's children—Chantal, Shane, and Gene.

All my grandchildren have been very supportive, calling frequently just to talk. Now that I am alone, Matthew likes to sleep over at my house. It's wonderful to have him.

Our extended Stein family expanded rapidly in Toronto with the immigration of my late brother Morris's wife, Miriam, and three of her daughters. In no time, it seemed, we were close to thirty people at the dinner table when the holidays arrived or at special family get-togethers: Lola and I, Mike, Pam, and their four children; David, Jana, and their three children; two of Linda's children, Lara, Warren, later joined by Warren's wife, Kim; my sister-in-law Miriam and her three daughters: Marsha and her husband Russell Jacobson; Dalya and her husband, Soren Dumrath, and their two children; and Batya.

Subsequently, Russell Jacobson's brother Bradley also moved to Toronto with his wife, Robyn, and their two children. Unfortunately, soon after Bradley's arrival, tragedy struck the Jacobson family back in South Africa. Their other brother, Gavin, was shot and killed in Durban.

As Mike had predicted when he came to Toronto in the early 1980s—the first Stein family member to do so—the others followed soon after.

❖ ❖ ❖

When I went off to study medicine in the late 1930s, I lost touch with many of my friends in Durban as they too went their own ways. When war broke out, some enlisted and went to North Africa to fight. Some, like Philly Friedman and Willy Hershovitz, never came home. It was only when I finally returned to Durban in March 1953, to open up my own practice and settle down, that I could re-establish old contacts and resume old friendships. From my own age group—school chums like Eric Shandel, Stanley Hackner, Mickey Schaffer, and Jackie Schaffer—some had moved on to other parts of the country, in particular, to Johannesburg. I then became friendly with a younger group, although, at this stage in our lives, a difference of two or three years in age was hardly as significant as it was when we were in grade school. In this group were Gerald Hackner, my cousin, Morris Schaffer and his brother Jackie, Markie Davidson, Abe Dubin, Gunter Lazarus, Bernhard Lazarus, Reggie Berkovitz, his brother Eddy, Alan Benn, Peter Ditz, Alan Magid, who subsequently became a judge of the Supreme Court of South Africa, and Martin Steinberg. As time went on, the circle widened. It included Charles Kluk, Garvin and Harold Bernstein, and Alec Ragoff, who became President of South Africa's Chamber of Commerce and Chancellor of the University of Natal.

We were an exceptionally close-knit, loyal group. We attached a high priority to protecting and maintaining one another's well-being. It is no overstatement to say, however, that I was perhaps the greatest beneficiary of that high standard we held as our group's priority. For it was only through the kindness of people like Gerald Hackner, Morris Schaffer, and Martin Steinberg that I could acquire enough money to retire in Canada. They made sure to include me in some of their investments and other financial endeavours. I am sure they did not need my limited contributions in any of their syndicates in order to make their investments viable. But they always called to offer me the chance to join their business deals. Gerald's generosity toward me began early—when I had just opened my practice in Durban, he did my books free of charge.

The depth of our friendships was heartening to Lola and me. The love and mutual respect we felt for our friends were evident when Lola and I celebrated our fiftieth wedding anniversary in 1995 in Toronto. Many of them made the substantial effort to travel from South Africa to share the occasion with us.

It pleases me a great deal, too, that so many of the friendships Lola and I made in the course of my long professional career have also held fast. Every year, for example, we receive a New Year's greeting card signed by the senior nurses of the hospital in which I worked some forty years ago.

To be remembered, despite one's shortcomings, is humbling and gratifying.

*"Mannie was one of the most outstanding surgeons
I have ever come across. He wouldn't operate until he had
fully prepared... He was also very good at explaining the issues
to his patients, to whom he showed warmth, understanding,
and respect."*
—SYD COHEN, AUGUST 2001

CHAPTER 18 **Credo**

LOOKING BACK OVER the four score and more years of my life, I shake my head almost in disbelief at the great many blessings that God has conferred upon me, even to this very day. Though I am not a religious man, I am not irreligious either; nor am I ungrateful, nor unaware that my life has been one of great personal happiness and professional privilege.

As a surgeon, I always tried to treat my patients kindly. A doctor is not merely a technician. One must combine science and art. It is never enough be a scientist; one must know how to talk to one's patient. First and foremost, that means one must actually care deeply about one's patient.

In medical school we were taught the sanctity of the Hippocratic oath. It was paramount every single day of my practice. In a paper entitled "Thoughts on Euthanasia" that I delivered at a symposium in Durban in 1978, and subsequently published by Oxford University Press in the collected proceedings of the symposium, I said the following about the ethics that must guide a doctor in his practice:

The doctor bases his moral and ethical standards on the Hippocratic oath. It says nothing about preserving life as such. It merely says, "So far as power and discernment shall be mine, I will carry out regimen for the benefit of the sick and will keep them from harm and wrong..."

The Hippocratic oath undertakes two things: to relieve suffering and to prolong and protect life. Where the patient is in the grip of a fatal and agonizing disease, the two may be in conflict. However, if by relieving suffering with drugs or other means, life is shortened, I do not believe it is the same as shortening life by deliberately killing the patient...

A medical practitioner is forbidden to destroy life. Nevertheless abortions are now legal in many parts of the world and legal in most parts under certain conditions. Further, during childbirth the child may be sacrificed for the sake of the mother. The utter corruption of medical ethics in Nazi Germany shows how the economic welfare of the State takes priority over the doctors' responsibility to the individual. In Germany, extermination of the physically, mentally and socially unfit was generally accepted. State Hospitals were required to furnish the names of patients who had been ill for five years or more and were unable to work. Such persons were often liquidated by order of the State. Two hundred and seventy-five thousand persons were put to death in charitable foundations for institutional care. What is terrifying are the relative values of a single concrete individual and the abstract State. One can even foresee an efficiency expert doing a ward round with a Chief of the Ward and deciding who shall live and who shall die. Perhaps this is over-simplification, but it bears consideration. It is a doctor's duty to ease pain and suffering. He must not destroy even a useless, painful life; nor must he prolong such a death.

Helping me to apply the strict tenets of the Hippocratic oath were the values I absorbed, and tried to incorporate into my medical practice, from Jewish traditions. I always regarded Maimonides as something of a medical role model. He was a scholar, philosopher, codifier of laws, and a very thoughtful, famous physician who lived in the twelfth century. Maimonides' prayer of the physician is often quoted as a sort of supplement to the Hippocratic oath. A rationalist par excellence, Maimonides believed very strongly that human beings had to harness all of their intellectual and scientific abilities to fight illness, to beat back the monsters of disease with reason, and to prevent ill health wherever possible with prudence and common sense. He abhorred reliance upon amulets and superstitions. To Maimonides, the patient was an entirety, a universe in and of itself. A physician had to take a comprehensive, not compartmentalized, view of the human being who stood before him or her in need of help and relying upon his or her expertise and judgment. His prayer is as follows:

"O Lord...Preserve me from the temptation of allowing myself to be influenced in the exercise of my profession by the thirst for gain or the pursuit of glory. Strengthen my heart so that it may be ever ready to serve both poor and rich, both friend and foe, both just and unjust.

"Help me to see only the man in the sufferer. Keep my mind clear in all circumstances, for great and sublime is the science that aims at preserving the health and life of all creatures."

I believe deeply in Maimonides' prayer, in his credo for serving the sick and the ill. I operated on a patient with the single hope of making the patient better. Otherwise I would not and did not do it. The patient always came first. The patient came before the staff, which, sometimes, got me into difficulty with the people I worked with. In a certain sense, the patient even came before my family. Sometimes this occasioned hardship for, but, I hope, never resentment in, the members of my family.

I once had a patient who was a Seventh Day Adventist. She had had a hysterectomy performed by a gynecologist earlier in the day. When I was asked to check on her in the evening, she was as white as a sheet. She was obviously losing a lot of blood. A ligature had come off the main artery to the ovary that had been removed. If we didn't operate on her immediately, if we didn't give her blood, she would die. But her husband refused any intervention. "It's the will of God," he told me firmly, without emotion.

I phoned my friend Solly Miller who was then a judge of the Court of Appeal. I needed to consult with him. My duty to my conscience, to my oath, was in profound conflict with the religious principles of my patient's husband. I needed legal, if not moral, guidance.

"By law, you can't do anything," Solly told me. "But I know what I would do."

He didn't explicitly tell me what to do. He did not have to. But I understood him very well. I immediately took the woman into the operating theatre, opened her up, fixed the problem and gave her thirteen pints of blood. She survived the procedure and neither she nor her husband ever complained. In fact, two years later, she returned to me for surgery on her varicose veins. The patient's life came first.

One time, while I was walking toward the operating room, a surgeon who had been performing an orthopedic procedure ran up to me in a state of understandable agitation, shouting that his patient had just suffered cardiac arrest in the middle of her surgery. He couldn't get her heart going. I rushed into the theatre, still wearing my street clothes.—there was no time to gown or scrub. I removed my jacket, picked up a scalpel, and opened the patient's chest. I pushed my hand into the cavity through the chest, found the heart, pumped it, massaged it, and finally got the heart going again.

I was covered in blood, but I felt that I had had no choice. I am not sure if most doctors today would have acted similarly because, if the wound had become septic, or if the patient had not survived the intervention, the doctor would probably have been sued.

I did not even consider the possibility of a lawsuit. The patient came first.

From this retrospective vantage point, almost eighteen years after I retired, there are a number of special achievements that leave me with a feeling of having contributed something good and lasting to the benefit of the wider society.

It gives me great satisfaction that I introduced vascular surgery to Durban in 1958, when I was thirty-eight years old. Professor Jannie Louw had performed the first graft of an aneurysm of the aorta in Cape Town in 1957 and I followed him less than a year later in Durban. There was nobody in Johannesburg at that time who was capable of doing these procedures. They appeared a year later.

In 1967, I helped Cyril Kaplan and A. G. Sweetapple establish a workers' compensation hospital in Durban. The three of us went to J. P. Grobbelaar, the Workmen's Compensation Commissioner for South Africa, to appeal to him to establish such an institution. He was amenable to the idea, but told us we would have to make it happen.

So we did.

We approached F. E. Balcan, the chairman of St. Augustine's Hospital, to ask the hospital's board to consider creating within its precincts a hospital for workers' compensation cases. They agreed to set aside an existing ward of the hospital for these cases on an interim basis.

Eventually, a separate workers' compensation wing was added to the hospital. We helped to design it. We helped ensure that it would be completed and supplied with the most modern of excellent equipment. The hospital allowed the newly built wing to be used rent-free for ten years, at which time unencumbered ownership of the building reverted to the hospital.

At first, the hospital treated white patients only, but this quickly changed and the facility became integrated for both black and white patients. After a time, the hospital became self-sufficient. Cyril Kaplan and I were on the founding board of directors and I stayed on the board for many years, even after I retired. We directed the rehabilitational programs at the hospital, which included a day clinic. No beds were needed; it was a therapeutic, treatment hospital.

In 1984, I was appointed by F. C. Clarke, Minister of Health for the Province of Natal, to be a one-man commission of inquiry "to investigate the short, medium, and long-term future of the Children's Hospital attached to Addington Hospital." The investigation entailed numerous interviews, discussions, the examination of records and demographic projections, research, and study. I concluded that the province must maintain the hospital as a viable institution and must also admit black children.

The health care debate rages in Canada. In the fourteen years I have lived here, there have already been a number of federal commissions and provincial committees examining the viability of the health care system. Indeed, even now, a federal commission of inquiry under the chairmanship of former Saskatchewan Premier Roy Romanow recently brought forward its own recommendations regarding the health care system. All the investigations ask one central question: How can we ensure a high standard of health care that does not bankrupt the treasury?

I don't know exactly what the best health care system is. I believe that universal access to high quality health care is one of the most vital markers of a humane and decent society. But I also believe that universal access to uniformly identical health care for each and every person is unrealistic and is not achievable. It may cause more grief than it prevents.

I have seen the changes in the delivery of health care throughout the world, in South Africa, Great Britain, Europe, the United States. The most successful systems have all been some variation on a dual system in which public and private components are blended.

Compared to most other parts of the world, Canada is a secure, non-violent society. An important part of what makes Canadian society so safe and secure is its health care system. Without the type of health care system that exists in Canada, even with all its problems, we could not have lived here, given the complicated nature of Lola's medical problems and the kind of care she required. The United States would have been totally unaffordable.

Physicians work by their oath to relieve suffering and to prolong and protect life. Some of us also work by Maimonides' prayer to "strengthen our heart so that it may be ready to serve both poor and rich, both friend and foe, both just and unjust." For society to enable its physicians and other health care providers to honour the oath and the prayer, there has to be a balance, in my view, between private and public health care.

Epilogue

IT WAS ONLY IN FEBRUARY 2002, some four months after Lola passed away, that I could finally face up to travelling again. And so, after some coaxing from Linda, I decided to travel to Durban to visit her and Tony. I hadn't been back there for ten years—Lola and I were last in South Africa in 1992, at which point she had already been on dialysis for a year.

I was glad for my decision to go because the visit was unforgettable. My friends rallied around me, wining and dining me morning, noon, and night. I was so occupied I hardly had time to think. Even Rabbi Zekry welcomed me back effusively when I went to shul the first Friday night I was there.

But it was hard not to notice two significant changes since my last stay there in 1992.

South Africa is now a black country. That may sound wildly trite and exceedingly obvious, but I say it as someone who lived there for more than six decades when, despite the overwhelming majority of its black population, it was a white country. Today, it is administered and governed by its black majority. With a population of forty million blacks and five million whites, that is as it should be.

That the transformation in the country's identity from white to black occurred so peacefully can only be attributed to Nelson Mandela.

The second change I noticed, however, was the proliferation of high fences and iron gates and the ubiquitous presence of security guards. I am afraid that when Mandela passes on, the situation in South Africa may deteriorate to be more like that of its neighbours. Time will tell. The challenges and the crises in South Africa are many. I give credit to the men and women who are striving to solve them.

❖ ❖ ❖

Perhaps no one has seen sadness and tragedy unexpectedly jolt people's lives more than a surgeon. We always intervened to try to save life, but not all of our interventions succeeded. We could never fully explain the reasons to the family members who were crushed by our "failures." We could only try to strengthen them for the road they would now have to travel diminished in some way. We understood the inevitability of sorrow because we saw it so often. And those of us who reflected on things also understood that the measure of our fulfillment and satisfaction depended on the way we lived our lives in between those sorrows.

Even though I was her father, and a doctor who spent the greater part of every day fighting disease, I was helpless to protect Linda, and her children, from the disease that took her first husband's life and from the unutterable sorrow that followed. It was a terrible time and there was no solace or comfort to be found. No words could abate so unabatable a loss. But in the midst of the sorrow was a small, handwritten note from Lara to her mother: "Don't cry, Mommy. God will look after us." Like the innocent, unselfconscious chirping of a delicate sparrow after a storm, Lara's little voice gave us strength. It reminded us that the imperative of all life is, simply, to live, to go forward, even when it is so very hard to do so. I held on to that note and read it back to Lara at her wedding twenty years later.

At Lola's funeral, the long wooden bench pews in the chapel were filled with friends and family, mourners and well-wishers all. Somehow the children and I managed to crowd into a single bench at the very front. Lola's coffin was barely inches from us. I sat at the end of the bench closest to the coffin.

Just before the memorial service began, twelve-year-old Jason walked across the front of the row and nudged his strong, young frame in beside me, between me and the edge of the bench. It was a tight squeeze and he could not have been too comfortable in that cramped space, but he remained there throughout the entire service. The whole time until we had to stand up for the *El Maleh Rachamim*, he inclined his head upon my left shoulder. Occasionally he reached out to hold my arm, nestling his right hand between my left arm and my body. He held on to me. We held on to each other.

Now, as I write these words, we are on the eve of Jason's bar mitzvah. The thought that Lola will not be there is deeply painful. Once again, there are neither words of solace nor of comfort.

But I recall the tenderness of Jason's gesture toward me and, in a profound way, toward the memory of Lola too. His affection flowed from the touch of his hand on my arm and from the gentle weight of his head on my shoulder.

It was his "note" to me, saying, as Lara had said to her mother," Don't cry, Grandpa, God will look after us...Don't cry, Grandpa, God will look after Granny too."

Appendix

Eulogy by Pam Medjuck-Stein for Lola Stein, October 4, 2001

Lola Stein was a gracious, loving, and truly happy woman. God gave her all she wished for; many wonderful years with the love of her life, Mannie, in a marriage made in heaven, three happy healthy children, Linda, Michael, and David, and twelve adoring and adorable grandchildren. Her illness may have defined her death, but her loving spirit and her great sense of humour defined her life.

Lola Jankelson was born in Butterworth, South Africa, the second of three sisters. She was an excellent student and left Pretoria, where her family had settled, to enter the School of Pharmacy in Durban at the age of eighteen. She endured the long hours of daily apprenticeship followed by rigorous evening classes, experiencing the discomfort of being the only female student in her year. In 1943 in South Africa it was a significant achievement for a young Jewish woman to graduate as a pharmacist.

Lola married Mannie on October 14, 1945, in a double wedding with her sister Annette and the late Max Melmed. Three months later, Lola and Mannie boarded a troop ship bound for London. Mannie's father's government connections had finagled tickets for them to travel with troops and previously evacuated British women and children returning to England at the close of the war. Mannie slept on a hammock five levels below deck and Lola shared a compartment with five others up above. Lola told me the adventure overseas with her new husband was very exciting. Mannie remembers that he was very sick.

They lived two and a half years abroad while Mannie specialized and trained first in London, then in Edinburgh, and finally in Dublin. Food was still rationed and they had to pump shillings into the gas heaters to warm themselves in the boarding-house rooms where they lodged. Nonetheless her memories of that time described the romance of being young and adventuresome in a Europe happy to be at peace. She spoke of the congeniality of all the students and the bicycles and the cheap picnics. I loved her stories of those days.

Lola and Mannie returned to South Africa late in 1948. He was looking for a job and she was pregnant with their daughter, Linda. In total, they moved twenty-five times during their marriage. She never complained about moving house. She took it as her task to create a beautiful and happy family life for Mannie and Linda and the two boys that followed. And she continually excelled.

Lola's *yahrzeit* will forever be on the first night of the holiday of Sukkot. In our tradition, one of the special things about Sukkot is the tribute the holiday holds for our matriarch Sarah, the first Jewish mother. Another element of Sukkot, closely linked, is holiday's emphasis on hospitality and happy celebration. Simply put, these are quintessentially the central elements of Lola; motherhood, hospitality, and celebration.

She supported her three children with a steady and unconditional love. She opened her home to Linda who was widowed early with three very young children and then embraced Linda's second husband, Tony, who was also widowed early. His two young children immediately became her beloved grandchildren. She let Michael leave for Israel at the age of seventeen even though she cried privately for him for six months before and a year after he left. She encouraged David to follow his ambitions and take his wife and three sweet babies to live in Europe even though she couldn't bear to see them go.

Lola had an ability to love that was beautiful and rare. Each of her twelve grandchildren believes that he or she was Lola's special child. She communicated her devotion and adoration to each child in a way that each felt unique and special. She was perceptive and sensitive to the individuality of each child.

Each grandchild was like one of her beloved flowers. She told me once to look closely at two roses and I would see that they are not at all the same. She would spend hours and hours arranging each beautiful flower in precisely the right place, just as she would ponder months ahead about what would be the perfect birthday gift for each grandchild, or the right Christmas gift for each nurse at the Sheppard Dialysis clinic, or each friend's anniversary gift. Her devotion to others was not general, but rather a collection of autonomous devotions.

Years ago, she'd take her Israeli nieces, then in Durban, on secret shopping trips for new clothes and milkshakes. She was generous to her sisters and their families quietly, constantly giving to them and never expecting or wanting anything back.

She loved to have fun. She would slip 20-rand notes to Warren as a young boy to play the horses, saying he could keep it if he won and she'd give him more if he lost. She would earnestly beg Jason to play and play again for her when he was a very squeaky six-year-old violinist. Then she'd ask Mannie for a whiskey. She would bake and decorate big gooey cakes with Matthew and Liane, allowing them to cover the cakes with every candy in the house and then serve the creations on Friday nights and expect us to eat it.

Her caring and mothering continued even during her years of illness, calling her family and friends around the world, just to stay in touch and to make sure they were all okay. She called Israel when bombs went off and when they didn't. She called if someone was ill. She called for a *simcha* and she called for a sadness. She called just to say, "Hello, Mannie and I are thinking of you." She loved all her many friends all these years deeply and with the fresh enthusiastic friendship of a schoolgirl.

I asked her recently why she never ever complained about the condition that tied her first to North America, then to Toronto, then to a wheelchair, and finally to bed. She said that people who complain are people who don't really care about those around them. She never wanted to darken anyone's day by saying she didn't feel good. After seven decades of dedication to a circle of family and friends unmatched by many, and the best part of another decade staving off illness, Lola is at rest. We have her beautiful smile now in photographs. Her indomitable spirit is with all of us.

My little Liane told me that when she thinks of Granny now her thoughts are half dark and sad that Granny is gone and half sparkly and shining that Granny is now peaceful and well. That's exactly how it is.

Lola, we will love you forever and remember you always.